A RESOURCE GUIDE TO
Public School Early Childhood Programs

EDITED BY CYNTHIA WARGER

Association for Supervision
and Curriculum Development
125 North West Street
Alexandria, VA 22314-2798

Printed in the United States of America

Typeset by Scott Photographics, Inc.
Printed by Edwards Brothers, Inc.

Ronald S. Brandt, *ASCD Executive Editor*
Nancy Modrak, *Manager of Publications*
René Townsley, *Associate Editor*

ASCD Stock No. 611-88036
ISBN 0-87120-151-8
Library of Congress
    Catalog Card No. 88-070536

$11.95

A Resource Guide to Public School Early Childhood Programs

Foreword

The children are the future and young children are its promise. It is therefore imperative that we focus attention on early childhood education.

Most of our concerns today center around painful, daily problems: how to raise students' scores from the bottom quartile, improve student attendance, and end the destructive cycle of low-achieving students. Poor achievers, the group most in need of consistent instruction, are the most likely group to be frequently absent, causing them to fall further and further behind. This cycle leads to the verifiable prediction that most of these students will drop out.

As a result, we have focused on preventing dropouts and the shocking end result. While this focus is important, it has been as effective and elusive as working to cure rather than prevent cancer. The greatest hope for change lies in investing in those at the beginning of the system to break the chain of failure.

The educational experimentation of the 1960s and early '70s are indicators of the dramatic difference that early childhood education can have. Since the pioneering studies of Benjamin Bloom on the essential need for education of 3- and 4-year-olds, additional studies have continued to document the academic and social success of those who have been involved in early education programs. In 1986, the High/Scope Educational Research Foundation issued findings[1] which verify that successful early childhood programs affect children's later success in school. This compelling research links student achievement in high school and beyond with the home and school as powerful influences on young children's intellectual development.

National reports also continue to stress the importance of early childhood education. Most recently, *The Forgotten Half: Non-College Youth in America*, a 1987 report by the Commission on Youth and

---

[1] L.J. Schweinhart, D.P. Weikart, and M.B. Larner, "Consequences of Three Preschool Curriculum Models Through Age 15," *Early Childhood Research Quarterly* 1 (1986): 15-45.

America's Future,[2] targets young children in its recommendations. The report calls for funds to serve an increasing percentage of the now unserved 3- to 5-year-olds.

As states increasingly mandate and fund preschool and kindergarten programs, the identification of sound philosophies and structures for those programs is essential. ASCD has taken the initiative in this book, dedicated to the promise of all young children and what must be done to guarantee their future and ours through academic success.

MARCIA KNOLL
ASCD President, 1987-88

---

[2]Published by the William T. Grant Foundation, 1001 Connecticut Avenue, N.W., Washington, DC 20036.

Introduction

CYNTHIA WARGER

American educators, encouraged by parents, political leaders, and public officials, have been moving quickly to accept new levels of responsibility for the education of young children. No longer the exclusive province of the very rich or very poor, preschool education now holds the potential for greater academic achievement, less at-risk behavior in the teen years, and enhanced educational opportunity for children from all economic sectors. This promise, combined with simple economic need, has led to heightened interest in programs designed by public school systems to prepare children for entry into the educational system.

Given the goal of providing young children with a solid foundation for later learning, public school leaders are charged with determining how their early childhood programs for 4- and 5-year-olds should be designed and what types of curriculum, instruction, and supervision to use. In this book, early childhood authorities assist us in identifying the trends, research, and issues that are at the heart of these important decisions.

The Preschool Curriculum Debate

Questions about the overall effectiveness of early childhood programs have given way to those focusing on the effectiveness of specific types of curriculum and teaching practices. There are real differences in opinion among professionals as to what constitutes an appropriate curriculum for young children; the most controversial issues center on academic versus developmentally appropriate curriculum and teacher-directed versus child-initiated instruction. For educators, these debates boil down to two questions: What should children be doing, and how should they be taught?

Since the 1960s, a succession of achievement-oriented education models have been designed to help children get ready for school. Across the country today, the tendency is toward instituting highly structured, academic programs in the preschool (Kagan

1988). Curriculums once intended for 1st grade have been moved to kindergarten and now are being moved into preschool. The assumption is that mastering a preacademic curriculum will give young children an early jump on the academic curriculum they will face later on. In fact, pressure from parents and the community to demonstrate that children are actually learning has led many programs to emphasize academic skill development with paper-and-pencil activities.

An emphasis on formal academic schooling for young children is not without its critics. Elkind (1986), for one, does not necessarily equate quality in programming with academic proficiency. He argues that there are distinct risks to an academically oriented program, among them the short-term risk of excessive stress and the long-term risks of decreased motivation and poor intellectual and social development. Other critics argue that young children must be offered opportunities to learn that are consistent with their levels of development; that curriculum must provide for all areas of the child's development, including physical, emotional, social, and cognitive; and that educational experiences should be child-initiated and match children's abilities and interests.

There are, of course, no clear-cut criteria for making an easy choice between one curriculum approach or the other. Both sides have evidence and arguments supporting their claims. Nevertheless, our public school leaders must make decisions now. They cannot wait for all the evidence to roll in.

The Purpose of This Book

The purpose of this book is to illuminate issues and concerns that surround the decisions administrators and teachers must make regarding their preschool programs. To that end, this book provides insights from several experts on the theory, research, and practice of preschool education.

Barbara Day provides a comprehensive overview of current preschool practices. Her chapter, which describes demographics and trends, explains what is happening across the country and leaves readers with an understanding of the challenges of providing a high-quality program.

Lilian Katz addresses what young children *should* be doing in light of development theory and contemporary research on children's intellectual and social development. She argues for an intellectually oriented approach and offers educators a model for organizing the curriculum.

The resistance to developmentally appropriate educational practice is the theme of David Elkind's chapter. From his perspective, providing developmentally appropriate learning experiences to young children actually presents a challenge to the values and beliefs represented by the existing public school establishment.

The next two chapters offer two models of quality programs. David Weikart details the findings of the Perry Preschool Project, and Douglas Carnine produces evidence from his work with direct instruction with 5-year-olds. This section concludes with a discussion, prepared by the ASCD Policy Panel on Early Childhood Education, of the critical issues facing school leaders.

Part two of the book features descriptions of 19 public preschool programs that reflect different elements of quality programming and current practice. The book concludes with a listing of useful resources for educators, prepared by Dianne Rothenberg of the ERIC Clearinghouse on Early Childhood Education.

While the authorities in preschool education have much about which to disagree, it is easy to find common threads in all that they write. They all agree that age 4 to 5 is a very important period in the development of young minds. They all agree that preschool education is worth the investment of our money, resources, and time. And they all agree that the preschool curriculum decisions now being made by public school officials will have a significant and long-term effect on the education of our children.

References

Elkind, D. "Formal Education and Early Education: An Essential Difference." *Phi Delta Kappan* 67 (1986): 631-636.
Kagan, S.L. "Current Reforms in Early Childhood Education: Are We Addressing the Issues?" *Young Children* 43, 2 (1988): 27-32.

Part I

1
What's Happening in Early Childhood Programs Across the United States

BARBARA D. DAY

n recent years, early childhood education has captured the attention of our nation as never before. Preschool education has been singled out by the National Governors' Association as the key investment in education for state governments. The Committee for Economic Development (1985, 1987) has issued two reports with the message that there is no better or more important national investment than in preschool programs for our nation's economically disadvantaged children. States have responded to the call with phenomenal rapidity; the number of states sponsoring preschool programs has doubled since 1985.

At a time of such high interest and fast growth in establishing public programs for young children, it is important to carefully examine what's happening, why, and how we can effectively resolve the many issues surrounding public early childhood programs. In this chapter we look at where we are in public programs for 4- and 5-year-olds and explore the issues and challenges that will determine the future of public early childhood programs.

General Trends

Early childhood education, focusing here on public and private programs for children from 3 to 5 years old in the United States, is a growing enterprise. From 1970 to 1980 nursery school enrollments grew by 81 percent, and between 1980 and 1985, they grew another 25 percent (Snyder 1986). The percentage of 5-year-olds enrolled in kindergarten has increased from 70 to about 95 percent over the past 15 years (Sava 1987). The percentage of 3- to 5-year-olds enrolled in preprimary programs grew from 37 to 55 percent between 1970 and 1985, and the population of 3- to 5-year-olds has been growing since 1979 (Snyder 1986).

Today enrollment in pre-primary programs (i.e., public and private programs prior to entry in grade 1) is at an all-time high, and expected to increase during the 1990s. According to Department of Education estimates, nearly 6.5 million children are enrolled in pre-primary programs today, an increase of over 2 million since 1970 (Center for Education Statistics 1985). Of this number, an estimated 4 million are enrolled in public school programs (see Figure 1.1). Pre-primary enrollment of over 7 million children is projected for 1993, an increase of another half million children in the next six years.

In spite of such significant enrollment increases, there is a tremendous unmet need for preschool programs, particularly for children from low-income families. A look at Head Start Program data is discouraging. The Children's Defense Fund (1987) reports that Head Start currently serves only 16 percent (451,000) of the 2.5 million children who need Head Start services. That leaves over 2 million of our nation's most disadvantaged children unserved, a grim statistic that is unlikely to improve unless the federal government substantially increases Head Start funding.[1]

Current social, demographic, and economic trends tell us that today's unmet need for early childhood programs will increase not only among the poor, but also among children at all socioeconomic levels. The population of young children is growing at the same time the number of children under six with working mothers is increasing dramatically. For instance,

• From 1980 to 1986 the number of children aged 5 and under increased by 10.9 percent. There are now over 18 million preschoolers in the United States, more than at any time in the past 20 years (U.S. Bureau of Census, reported by Beach 1987).

---

[1]According to the Children's Defense Fund (1987), the $20 million Head Start funding increase proposed for FY 1988 is not enough to keep pace with inflation at the current service level, and the Follow-Through Program designed to support progress made by Head Start graduates in the elementary grades is slated for elimination in FY 1988.

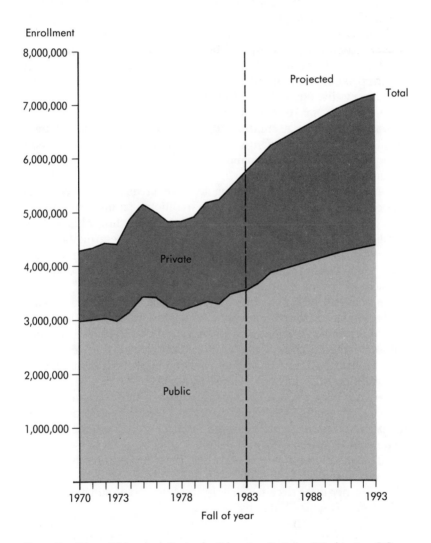

Figure 1.1
Preprimary Enrollment by Control of School

From *Condition of Education,* Center for Education Statistics (Washington, DC: U.S. Government Printing Office, 1985).

• According to 1985 U.S. Bureau of Census statistics, nearly half of all infants have working mothers. Fifty-nine percent of the mothers of 3- and 4-year-olds are employed outside the home, and nearly 70 percent of school-aged children have working mothers (Mitchell 1987, Zigler 1987).

• It has been projected that 9 out of 10 mothers—married or single—will be in the workforce by 1990 (McCormick 1986).

• In 1985 there were 9.6 million children under 6 with working mothers. By 1995 there will be 14.6 million children under 6 with working mothers (Children's Defense Fund 1987).

• By the year 2000, if current trends continue, 30 percent of U.S. women will delay childbearing until after age 30. These women are likely to be career-oriented and to reenter the workforce as soon as possible. They will demand and be able to pay for more and better child care (Lewis 1985).

A second trend contributing to the increasing need for preschool programs is the decline of the traditional family unit and the growing number of children living in single-parent households. Few families, whether the father is present or not, have a mother who stays at home to care for young children. For single-parent families with young children, the problem of poverty often compounds the problem of finding child care.

• Between 1960 and 1985 the percentage of traditional households decreased from 60 percent to 7 percent (Futrell 1987).

• Currently, 20 percent of all American children live in homes without fathers (Bennett 1987), and it is projected that 40 percent of all children will live in a female-headed household before reaching adulthood (Children's Defense Fund 1987).

• The poverty rate for families maintained by a woman with no husband present is 34 percent (Children's Defense Fund 1987), and the poverty rate for female-headed families with young children is 60 percent (Halpern 1987.)

The third trend is the enduring problem of poverty among young children.

• Twenty-five percent of all 4- and 5-year-olds today are poor (Children's Defense Fund 1987).

• One in 6 of all 4- and 5-year-olds today lives in a family where neither parent has a job (Children's Defense Fund 1987).

• Poor children are only half as likely to be enrolled in preschool programs as children from affluent families. While 67 percent of 4-year-olds from families with incomes over $35,000 are enrolled in preschool programs, less than 33 percent of 4-year-olds from families with incomes less than $10,000 are enrolled in preschool programs (Children's Defense Fund 1987).

These trends add up to a tremendous challenge for our nation in terms of providing for the education and care of our young children. In spite of the sobering statistics, many positive steps are being taken to meet the needs of our 4- and 5-year-olds.

What's Happening in Early Childhood Programs for 5-Year-Olds

Kindergarten Trends

Today about 95 percent of all 5-year-olds are enrolled in kindergarten programs (Sava 1987), making universal education for 5-year-olds for all practical purposes a reality. Public school programs serve the large majority of kindergarten-aged children. The Department of Education estimates that 2.5 million 5-year-olds are enrolled in public pre-primary programs as opposed to 0.5 million in private schools (Center for Education Statistics 1985). As of 1986, 46 states provided kindergarten programs for over 90 percent of the eligible population (Robinson 1987).

In addition to the trend toward universally available kindergarten education, four other major trends in public kindergarten programs have been identified (Robinson 1987):

Local funding and control of kindergarten programs. Local districts in 14 states provide a significant portion of kindergarten funding. In many states, the focus of the curriculum, the birthdate deadline for entrance, and the length of the kindergarten day are local decisions.

Programs are offered a minimum of two to three hours per day. While half-day (2-3 hour) programs are most common, the majority of states cited the 2-3 hour range as a *minimum* requirement; eight states reported providing a 4-6 hour day; and 14 states reported a range of from 2.5-6 hour programs where local districts provided funds to exceed minimum state requirements. These findings are consistent with results from the 1986 Educational Research Service (ERS) national survey of kindergarten policies and practices.

Kindergarten teachers tend to hold college degrees. In 28 states the minimum requirement for kindergarten teachers is a bachelors degree; in 11 states over 20 percent of the kindergarten teachers hold master's degrees.

Attendance at age 5 is compulsory in some states. Seven states required kindergarten attendance in 1986, as opposed to only one state in 1982. However, given the current level of kindergarten enrollment of 5-year-olds at about 95 percent, legislation mandating attendance would be little more than a political statement.

Kindergarten Program Priorities

According to the 1986 ERS survey of 1,200 kindergarten principals, preparation for school and children's social, emotional, and language development received more attention than academic achievement. The majority of principals (62.6 percent) responding to the survey indicated that the primary focus of their kindergarten programs was preparation (academic/social readiness); 22 percent gave primary focus to academics (skills and achievement).

When asked to rate a list of 10 possible kindergarten priorities, principals gave high priority to several developmental areas. Over 80 percent ranked social and language development, and over 70 percent ranked emotional development and self-discipline as high priorities. Over 50 percent of the principals ranked physical coordination/motor development, development of health/safety habits, and development of work/study habits as high priorities. Personality development was ranked high by 39.9 percent of the principals. Academic achievement was ninth on the list with 28.3 percent giving it a high ranking. The last was artistic expression, with 23.8 percent giving it high priority.

While we cannot assume that these data are indicative of nationwide kindergarten program policies and priorities, they do provide insight into what's happening in a substantial number of kindergarten programs. It appears from the principals' responses to the ERS Survey that they and their school districts appreciate the importance of developmental readiness for academic tasks. It is encouraging that such high percentages of principals ranked a wide range of developmental areas as high program priorities, even though only 8.1 percent indicated that their primary kindergarten focus is developmental.

Kindergarten Issues

The above data about kindergarten trends and program priorities are closely tied in with today's predominant issues in kindergarten programs: (1) What is the appropriate focus or purpose of kindergarten programs? and (2) Should kindergarten programs be full- or part-day?

The Purposes of Kindergarten. When kindergartens were first established in this country in the 19th century, they primarily served a social service rather than an educational function (Hill 1987). For many years kindergartens were operated mainly by private philanthropic organizations in response to the problems accompanying massive immigration and city slums. In this century, from the 1920s to the 1950s, kindergartens tended to be privately operated and attended by middle- and upper-class children. In those years, the primary function of the kindergarten was to provide a comfortable, child-centered group experience outside of the home (Connell 1987). Today most kindergartens are part of the public school system, serving children from all socioeconomic backgrounds. Their primary focus, if not academic achievement (which many would argue it is), is preparation for the academic tasks of the 1st grade.

The appropriateness of focusing on preparation for later academic tasks is a complex and debatable issue (Connell 1987, Hill 1987, and Carnine et al. in chapter 5 of this volume). The fundamental question concerns whether the child should be fitted to the curriculum or the curriculum fitted to the child. Our current system of arbitrarily organizing both the child and the curriculum into grade levels based on chronological age indicates that we have "accepted" the proposition of fitting the child to the curriculum. The implicit goal of each grade level, including kindergarten, is to "prepare" children for the academic tasks at the next level.

Our school systems' response to early school failure is indicative of how far we have gone to fit young children to the existing curriculum. Both post-kindergarten grade levels (often called transitional 1st grade or senior kindergarten) and special prekindergarten grades (often called junior kindergarten or developmental kindergarten) are based on the assumption that we must remediate children who are not ready for the curriculum prescribed for their age. The inefficiency of this practice is intuitively obvious, as is the tremendous cost in self-esteem to the children who are segregated in special programs.

Although prevailing practice indicates that the actual purpose of kindergarten is to prepare children for 1st grade, prevailing child development theory (National Association for the Education of Young Children 1986) indicates that such a purpose is inappropriate and counterproductive. Three of the basic tenets of child development research and practice (Day in press) are that:

• Children grow and develop at unique individual rates that are often unrelated to chronological age.

• Four- and 5-year-old children learn best through doing, through direct immediate involvement with the environment, and through sensory input of observation, manipulation, and experimentation.

• Four- and 5-year-old children are experiencing rapid and important growth in many developmental areas, including the cognitive/intellectual, psychosocial, and physical-motor domains.

According to the National Association for the Education of Young Children (NAEYC 1986) in its position statement on programs for 4- and 5-year-olds, the degree to which the program is based on principles of child development is a major determinant of program quality. NAEYC lists several implications of these principles for curriculum goals and teaching methods:

• Appropriate curriculums stimulate learning in all developmental areas: physical, social, emotional, and cognitive. Inappropriate curriculums narrowly focus on cognitive development without recognizing and supporting the interactive relationship among all areas of development.

• Appropriate curriculums respond to individual differences in ability, interests, development, and learning styles. Inappropriate curriculums expect all children to achieve the same narrowly defined skills within the same time frame.

• Appropriate programs offer children the choice of many learning activities. Children learn through active exploration and interaction with adults and other children; they are provided with concrete learning activities that are relevant to their own life experiences; and they work individually or in small, informal groups most of the time. In inappropriate programs, teachers direct almost all the activity. Children spend a large portion of their time passively sitting, listening, and waiting; and abstract learning materials such as workbooks, ditto sheets, and flashcards dominate a curriculum that emphasizes large-group, teacher-directed instruction and rote memorization and drill.

From NAEYC's perspective, fitting 4- and 5-year-olds to the traditional school curriculum (i.e., preparing them for the academic tasks of the 1st grade) is not the appropriate purpose of kindergarten programs. Hill (1987) has suggested that kindergarten has three important functions. The first and most important is to minister to the nature and needs of our 5-year-olds. Kindergarten should fit and meet their abilities, developmental level, learning styles, and interests. The second purpose is to lay the foundation for a good start in school subjects and activities. Kindergarten should establish the motivation and skills for success in school through developmentally appropriate activities, but not through a watered down version of 1st grade tasks. The third purpose is to provide comprehensive assistance with children's medical, nutritional, and psychological needs. In establishing the goals for our kindergarten programs, educators must recognize all three functions, rather than focusing on narrowly defined academic competencies.

Full-Day Versus Half-Day Programs. Inseparable from the purpose of kindergarten programs is whether public schools should provide full-day kindergarten programs. Some support full-day kindergarten for the purpose of providing much-needed quality child care, but oppose a full-day academic program. Others support full-day kindergarten programs for the purpose of providing the extra academic preparation and skills that children need to ensure success in school, but oppose a full-day for the purpose of providing child care.

The issue is further complicated by practical and philosophical child-rearing issues (Elkind 1987). For the many families with a single working parent or two working parents, a full day away from home is a practical necessity. For others, it is a philosophical question of whether or not they want their children away from home for a full day of education, care, both, or neither. By providing a full-day kindergarten program in which parents have the *choice* of enrolling their children for all or part of the day, the public school could enable parents to follow their own philosophies yet accommodate those parents who want or need full-day programs.

Much of the controversy with full-day programs tends to polarize around the issues of "education versus care" and "academic versus developmental focus." Education leaders can address these issues most effectively by focusing not on the polarities, but on our central purpose—serving the nature and needs of 5-year-old children.

For example, thinking in terms of "education *versus* care" inaccurately limits "education" to the acquisition of academic skills and knowledge and "care" to the provisions of custodial and protective services. As Bettye Caldwell (1986) noted, education and care are essentially inseparable: public schools already provide many services, such as nutritional programs and health screening, that could be considered care and protection, and quality day care programs include an educational component. Caldwell concludes, "In order for either service to be relevant to the needs of children and families, both components must be present" (p.38).

Likewise, the issue of academic versus developmental programs involves an inappropriately narrow view of the goals and actual impact of either program type. There is a very real difference in articulated goals; developmental programs explicitly focus on the "whole child" (social, emotional, physical, and cognitive development), whereas academic programs explicitly focus on cognitive and academic skills. The flaw in such a distinction is that regardless of the stated purpose and focus of a kindergarten program, the children involved are actually learning and developing in many areas, and the child's kindergarten experience and learning environment makes an impact on that development whether it is intentional or not.

It is more appropriate to focus our attention on the common goal of both program types: to provide the foundation and the motivation for successful lifelong learning. Kindergarten programs should incorporate academic content and skill development within a framework of individually appropriate experiential activities that provide opportunities to grow in all the important developmental areas. Such a program will result in both academic success and joy in learning (Day and Drake 1986).

Regarding the academic effects of full-day kindergartens, a number of studies indicate that full-time students exhibit stronger academic skills (Murray 1987). Murray concluded from a recent review of research that while there are no data to overwhelmingly support the all-day program, it appears that the full-day, every day model of attendance has an advantage from a pedagogical viewpoint. It is important to note that Murray's reference to a pedagogical viewpoint is not an endorsement of intensive academic programs. On the contrary, he indicates that overemphasis on academic skills is a potential disadvantage of full-day programs. Murray cites Uphoff and Gilmore's (1986) summary of several studies, which indicate that formal school for which young children are not developmentally ready creates long-term academic and social difficulties. According to Murray, the advantages of a full-day schedule are that it allows more time for the teachers to observe and assess children, to screen for potential learning problems, and to extend the curriculum to include more information and a variety of relaxed, unhurried experiences.

Murray's summary of the advantages of a full day are consistent with my own research and observations in kindergarten classrooms. A full day allows the time for ongoing individual evaluation and program planning which, in turn, enables teachers to offer each child a variety of developmentally appropriate experiential learning opportunities. Children in full-day classrooms with such opportunities exhibit an exceptionally high rate of engagement in learning tasks (Day and Drake 1986). What children need in order to attain optimal academic and developmental benefits is not an intensive program of any kind, but appropriate learning experiences woven throughout the day in a secure, unpressured environment.

What's Happening in Early Childhood Programs for 4-Year-Olds

The most recent and comprehensive information about public preschool programs comes from the Public School Early Childhood Study completed this year (Marx and Seligson 1987, Mitchell 1987a and 1987b). The study, a joint project of Wellesley College and Bank Street College, included three components:

• A state survey conducted by Wellesley College researchers (Marx and Seligson 1987) who collected information about state legislation and funding from officials in all 50 states. Most of their data apply to FY 88. A description of findings is found in Figure 1.2, pages 14-21.

• A school district survey (Mitchell 1987a, 1987b) that gathered information about the many types of programs serving children younger than 5 years in school districts across the nation. Over 1,200 districts supplied information about nearly 1,700 programs.

• Site visits conducted by Bank Street College researchers (Mitchell 1987a, 1987b).

Unless otherwise referenced, the data in this discussion are drawn from the Public School Early Childhood Study.

Preschool Trends

A predominant trend in public preschool programs is rapidly growing state involvement. For over 20 years, the federal government was the major provider of public preschool education through

Figure 1.2
State Initiatives in Early Childhood Education

STATE	POPULATION SERVED	HOURS OF OPERATION	NUMBERS SERVED
ALASKA enacted 1983	4-year-olds Head Start eligibility	half day 5 villages	45 children (FY87)
CALIFORNIA enacted 1966	4-year-olds at risk (low income; limited English)	half day, 185 contracts; 500+ sites	19,221 children (FY88)
DELAWARE enacted 1986	4-year-olds disadvantaged children targeted	half day 3 pilot programs (FY88)	99 children (FY88)
FLORIDA state funds used to supplement migrant program since 1981	3- and 4-year-olds migrant children	full day	2,579 children (FY86)
FLORIDA enacted 1986 begun 1986-87	3- and 4-year olds targeted at risk only	half or full day including full working day; 19 districts (FY88)	1,000 children (FY88)
ILLINOIS enacted 1985 begun Jan. 1986	3- 5-year-olds at risk of academic failure	half or full day 97 programs (FY88)	7,400 children (FY87)
KENTUCKY enacted 1986	3- and 4-year olds "at risk"	half and full day PACE (FY87-88) 12 districts 18 classrooms; 4 programs EIG (Education Innovative Grant)	270 PACE (FY87-88) 366 EIG (FY87-88)

Source: F. Marx and M. Seligson, "Draft Notes on States' Findings from the Public School Early Childhood Study" (Wellesley, Mass.: College Center for Research on Women, 1987).

RESOURCES	RATIOS	ECE TRAINING	METHOD OF FUNDING
$197,000 (FY88) $250,000 (FY87)	unknown	unknown	targeted grants for Head Start like programs
$35.5 million (FY88 estimate)	1:10		reimbursement on average daily attendance; contracts with school district, which may subcontract; grants may also go directly to private nonprofits
$189,000 (FY88)	1:8	unknown	competitive grants school districts only
$2.9 million (FY88)	1:10	no	districts may subcontract to nonprofits; 60% state funds, 40% federal
$1.6 million (FY88)	local option 1:10 recommended	yes	project grants to school districts; may subcontract
$12.7 million (FY88)	local option 1:8 preferred	yes	project grants; up to one per district no local match; may subcontract to nonprofits
$900,000 PACE (FY88) $267,703 EIG (FY87-88)	1:7.5 PACE unknown EIG	no PACE unknown EIG	competitive grants to school districts; EIG may be subcontracted, PACE eligibility based on district with 60% or more adults without a high school diploma

Figure 1.2 continued.
State Initiatives in Early Childhood Education

STATE	POPULATION SERVED	HOURS OF OPERATION	NUMBERS SERVED
LOUISIANA enacted 1985 begun fall, 1985	4-year-olds at risk	most full day 50 out of 66 districts 71 classes (FY88)	1,272 children (FY88)
MAINE Head Start expansion enacted 1984	4-year-olds at risk Head Start requirement	most half day some 2 days/week 13 programs	724 children (FY88)
MAINE enacted 1984	4-year-olds	half day 5 districts (FY88)	167 children
MARYLAND enacted 1979	4-year-olds at risk	half day 15 districts 72 classes (FY88)	2,820 children (FY88)
MASSACHUSETTS enacted 1985 begun fall, 1986	3- 5-year-olds low income	half or full day including full working day 121 programs (FY87) 56 pre-K and day care	N/A
MICHIGAN pilot project began Jan., 1986	4-year-olds at risk	most half day 23 programs (FY87)	800 children (FY87)
MICHIGAN enacted 1987	4-year-olds living in districts meeting funding formula requirements	half day	N/A
NEW JERSEY since 1903	4-year-olds	half day 93 school districts (FY86)	5,794 children (FY88)

RESOURCES	RATIOS	ECE TRAINING	METHOD OF FUNDING
$1.8 million (FY88)	1:10 with aide 1:15 without	no	project grants; up to 4 per district; no local match
$1.9 million (FY88)	1:7.5 (Head Start ratios)	HS requirement	formula allocations
N/A	none	no	school districts regular school aid formula
$3.3 million (FY88)	1:10	yes	project grants; selection based on low 3rd grade test scores
$10.3 million (FY88)	1:7.5	yes	competitive grants to districts; may subcontract; 75% of funds to low-income districts
$1.5 million (FY88)	1:10	no	project grants to school districts; 30% local match; may subcontract with private nonprofit
$10 million (FY88)	1:10	no	school districts only which meet state funding formula requirements
$6.9 million (estimated for 1989)	1:25	no, but most teachers have nursery school endorsement	school districts regular school aid formula

Figure 1.2 continued.
State Initiatives in Early Childhood Education

STATE	POPULATION SERVED	HOURS OF OPERATION	NUMBERS SERVED
NEW JERSEY enacted 1987 to begin Nov. 1987	3- 5-year-olds at risk; Head Start requirement	half or full day including full year, full working day	N/A
NEW YORK enacted 1966	3- and 4-year-olds 90% low income	most half-day 90 districts (FY88)	12,000 children (FY88)
OHIO enacted 1985-86	3- 5-year-olds	half or full day pilot models 8 districts (FY87)	N/A
OKLAHOMA enacted1980	4-year-olds	half or full day 35 districts (FY88)	1,400 children (FY88)
OREGON passed 1987 implemented 1988-89	4-year-olds 80% of children must meet Head Start eligibility	half day	unknown
PENNSYLVANIA since 1965	4-year-olds	half day 9 districts (FY87)	3,260 children (FY87)
SOUTH CAROLINA enacted 1984; Chapter I funding since 1971	4-year-olds with deficient "readiness" based on individual assessment	half day 86 districts, (FY88)	10,715 children (FY88)

RESOURCES	RATIOS	ECE TRAINING	METHOD OF FUNDING
$1 million (FY88)	1:10	yes	allocation by counties and competitive grants to programs; priority to Head Start programs but school districts and nonprofits may apply; 25% matching requirement
$27 million (FY88)	1:7.5	no	project grants via a proposal process; 10% local match; new program limited to half day only
$83,000 (FY88 estimate)	1:12	no	project grants via RFP to school districts; new programs half day only
$805,275 (FY88)	1:10	yes	project grants via RFP to school districts; maximum grant per district $27,000 (FY88); private schools may also apply
$1.1 million (FY88-89)	unknown	unknown	competitive grants to school districts, which may subcontract; direct contracts permitted
$1.7 million (FY87 estimate)	local option	unknown	state aid formula for kindergarten used
$10.9 million (FY88)	1:10 recommended	yes	allocation to districts based on students "not ready"; districts may subcontract

Figure 1.2 continued.
State Initiatives in Early Childhood Education

STATE	POPULATION SERVED	HOURS OF OPERATION	NUMBERS SERVED
TEXAS enacted 1984 began fall 1985	4-year-olds low-income or limited English proficiency	half day 405 districts (FY86)	48,800 children (FY87)
VERMONT enacted 1987	3- and 4-year-olds at risk, low-income; limited English proficiency; other handicapping conditions	half or full day including full work day	250 children (FY88 estimate)
WASHINGTON enacted 1985	4-year-olds Head Start eligibility	half day	2,000 children (FY88)
WASHINGTON, D.C. enacted 1968	4-year-olds	117 full day + 27 half day (FY87) 170 full day (FY88)	3,444 children (FY88)
WEST VIRGINIA programs operated since 1972*	3- and 4-year-olds at risk and low-income	half day and full day* 6 programs	215 children (FY86)
WISCONSIN enacted 1985	4-year-olds	half day 25 districts (FY87)	5,850 (FY88 estimate)

*School code revised in 1983 to permit local county school boards to establish prekindergarten programs for children under age 5. The programs listed are those not primarily for handicapped children.

RESOURCES	RATIOS	ECE TRAINING	METHOD OF FUNDING
$37.6 million (FY87) $64.5 million (FY88)	1:22	yes with exemptions	formula allocation; matching grant based on local property value
$500,000 (FY88) maximum $30,000 per grant	1:10	no	competitive grants based on RFP; preference to communities without other early childhood programs; grants to school districts, which may subcontract; direct contracts permitted
$6.1 million (FY88)	1:6	yes	competitive grants to school districts; Head Start and private non-profits
$12.2 million (FY88)	1:10 full day 1:15 half day	yes	local district regular school aid formula; used Chapter I funds prior to 1982
$258,574 (FY86)	1:15	yes	4 of the programs run by the DOE as fiscal agent; 2 are run by counties under contract with DOE
$4.3 million (FY88)	1:20 recommended	no local option	state aid formula to local districts; average local contribution is 52%

the Head Start program. As of 1986, Head Start had produced over 8 million graduates (Scarr and Weinburg 1986). In spite of its large number of graduates, Head Start now serves only a small percentage of eligible children, and expansion to serve more children is unlikely. Today, states are providing the impetus to expand existing programs and to create new programs for the nation's 4-year-olds.

Twenty-eight states are now funding or have committed to fund state prekindergarten programs, to supplement Head Start programs, or to provide parent education programs. This represents a phenomenal increase in a short amount of time. Only 4 states (California, New York, Pennsylvania, and New Jersey) have been funding preschool programs for more than 10 years (Morado 1986). Since 1985, 14 states have either initiated or expanded prekindergarten programs (Marx and Seligson 1987).

The amount of program funding as well as the number of children served vary considerably from state to state:

• The smallest state prekindergarten programs are in Alaska (funding $197,000, serving 45 children), Delaware (funding $189,000, serving 99 children), Ohio (funding $83,000, number served not available), Vermont (funding $500,000, serving 250 children), and West Virginia (funding $258,000, serving 215 children).

• The largest state programs are in Texas (funding $64.5 million, serving 48,000 children), California (funding $35.5 million, serving 19,111 children), and New York (funding $27 million, serving 12,000 children). Other leaders, each with a $10 million or more investment, are Illinois, Massachusetts, Michigan (tentative funding of $10 million), and South Carolina (funding $10.9 million, serving 10,715 children). Funding in the remaining states ranges from approximately $1 million to $7 million.

• Eight states allocate funds to supplement Head Start programs: Rhode Island, Alaska, Washington, Maine, Minnesota, Connecticut, Massachusetts, and the District of Columbia. Their contributions range from $0.4 million to $2.7 million.

As a whole, the state investments are an impressive and encouraging beginning for meeting the early childhood program needs of our 4-year-olds (about half the programs serve 4-year-olds only and half serve children ages 3-5).

A second significant trend in public preschool programming is the targeting of funding for children who are economically disadvantaged or academically at risk. The decision to target such children is not surprising in the absence of adequate funding to serve all. The Committee for Economic Development and the National Governors Association have effectively promoted public investments in programs for poor children and have persuasively presented the social and economic benefits not only for the children served, but for society at large.

The High/Scope Foundation has estimated a $7 savings for every $1 invested in high-quality preschool programs; on a broader scale, the Children's Defense Fund (1987) estimates a national savings of $10 billion in reduced costs of special education, repeated grades, delinquency, and other consequences of school failure, if Head Start were to provide services to every poor child 3 to 5 years of age (Children's Defense Fund 1987). We are far from serving all poor children through Head Start and the state programs combined. The Committee for Economic Development (1987) has estimated it would cost $3 billion annually to provide quality preschool programs for all our economically disadvantaged 4-year-olds. However, the states are moving in that direction by earmarking funding for the disadvantaged first.

The third trend in public preschool programming is the states' efforts to coordinate and use all available resources for young children efficiently and effectively. Almost all states have a coordinating body at the state level, and roughly half of the states allow for some form of contracting with appropriate public and private agencies to provide preschool programs or components of those programs. Such efforts, however, are incomplete and warrant further planning and action. Marx and Seligson (1987) note that no state has yet to fully coordinate funding for state prekindergarten and child care programs. Further, only one-third of the states require local level coordination, and in some cases lack of local coordination has resulted in competition for resources between state prekindergartens and Head Start programs. Since so many state initiatives are relatively new, it is likely that coordination will improve as we become more experienced in planning and administering state programs.

Preschool Programs

This section, on preschool program schedules and quality factors, includes information from both the aforementioned state and district surveys. The district survey included data about almost 1700 programs, categorized as Head Start, Chapter 1 Pre-K, Special Education, Locally-funded Pre-K, Summer Program, Nursery School Operated by High School Students, and Other. The most frequently occurring program types were Head Start (10.4 percent), Special Education (31.5 percent), State-funded Pre-K (15.2 percent), and Other (11.1 percent).

Program Schedules. State survey results show that 60 percent of state prekindergarten programs are half-day programs, and 25 percent are either half or full school days. Four states (Vermont, Massachusetts, New Jersey, and Florida) permit children to be served for the full working day. However, few full working day programs have been funded to date.

District survey data show that the typical operating schedule for all program types is 3-hour sessions offered every day of the school year schedule. The notable exception is child care programs that typically operate for 9 or more hours per day on a calendar year schedule.

Quality Factors in Preschool Programs. A major goal of the Public School Early Childhood Study was to gather information about program characteristics that determine program quality. Using standards developed in 1986 by the National Association for the Education of Young Children (NAEYC), the researchers identified five major ingredients in quality: (1) staffing patterns, (2) teacher qualifications, (3) comprehensive services, (4) curriculum, and (5) parent participation.

Staffing Patterns. Low staff-child ratios and small-group sizes are key components of quality preschool programs. NAEYC (1986) has established a staff:child ratio of 1:10 in a group no larger than 20 children as an acceptable staffing pattern. It was found in the state survey that only five states permit staff child ratios in excess of 1:10, and some states require lower ratios in their prekindergarten programs. In the district survey, the staffing patterns (mean group sizes and staff-child ratios) in all program types met or exceeded the NAEYC standard.

Teacher Qualifications. NAEYC (1986) recommends that teachers have college level specialized preparation in early childhood education, as well as supervised experience with young children before they are placed in charge of a group. According to the state survey report, about half the state programs require teachers to have training or certification or both in early childhood education.

Similarly, district survey results show that half of the programs require teachers to have early childhood certification, and almost three-quarters require a bachelor's degree. Unfortunately, two-thirds of the programs do not require previous experience for teachers. Actual hiring practices in the surveyed school districts often exceed the minimum certification requirements, with a little over half of the teachers hired having both certification and at least one year of experience teaching children younger than 5 years.

The district survey also addressed requirements for paraprofessionals, who are employed in 87 percent of the programs. Over half of the programs require a high school diploma for paraprofessionals, and experience is rarely required. About one-fifth of the paraprofessionals had both a year of early childhood training and at least one year of experience with young children.

Comprehensive Services. Another significant factor in program quality is comprehensive services, particularly since most of the programs are targeted to children who are economically disadvantaged or academically at risk. Comprehensive services include medical, social, and health services, among others; parent participation; and a program that addresses all areas (social, emotional, physical, and cognitive) of a child's development. Findings from the state survey indicate that about half of the states require comprehensive developmental programs. In the district survey, almost one-fifth of the children are enrolled in Head Start programs that are required to provide comprehensive services.

Curriculum. A curriculum based on principles of child development is the crucial determinant of program quality (NAEYC 1986). As mentioned above, half the state programs are required to provide comprehensive developmental programs. According to Marx and Seligson (1987), the states that do not require comprehensive developmental programs either have no curricular requirements or primarily focus on cognitive curriculum.

The Public School Early Childhood Study also took a close look at curriculum by visiting and observing programs in 13 different communities. Generally, early childhood curriculum models fall along a continuum from highly structured, teacher-directed, and cognitively focused programs (e.g., Bereiter and Englemann's 1966 direct instruction model) to unstructured, child-centered, and socially/emotionally focused models (e.g., traditional nursery schools). At the middle of the continuum are open-structure models that involve teacher- and child-initiated activities as well as teacher-structured individualized learning activities designed to achieve a balance of cognitive, social, emotional, and physical development goals. Examples of open structure curriculum models are the Montessori method, the High/Scope open framework model (Hohmann et al. 1979), and the developmental and experiential program described by Day and Drake (1983, 1986) and Day (in press). Curriculum models at the highly structured, cognitively focused end of the continuum are generally developmentally inappropriate for 4-year-olds; programs in the middle and at the unstructured child-centered end are generally developmentally appropriate. While the researchers found that some kind of curriculum was used in every site, there was wide variation in the appropriateness of curriculums.

Two case studies of the site visits contrast the range of variation (Mitchell 1987a, 1987b). The first type of curriculum is teacher-designed and involves many hands-on exploration and discovery activities for the children. In a typical science activity in this curriculum, the science teacher and children gather around a table on which ice cubes of different sizes and shapes, various containers, and paper towels are placed. The children feel the ice cubes and talk about how ice changes and melts. They experiment and explore changes, noting what happens to ice in water, what happens to ice wrapped in a towel, and so forth.

The second site uses a prescribed-skills mastery curriculum with highly structured teacher-directed lessons and no experiential or child-initiated activities. When conducting typical classroom activities, the teacher stands in front of a group of children, holds up a card with a letter printed on it, and calls on a child to identify the letter. In another part of the room, an aide sits at the blackboard in front of a group of children. The aide draws a shape on the board and then calls on a child to draw an identical shape and tell the name of the shape. A third group of students sits around a table independently putting together puzzles.

It is easy to imagine what very different ideas the children in the two settings are developing about the meaning and value of learning. Such a contrast vividly illustrates the importance of carefully considering the effects of our curriculum focus and methods. Curriculum planners are deciding what children will be experiencing and are, in fact, shaping the growth and development of those children (Leeper et al. 1984, p. 178). Researchers disagree about the long-term academic and social impact of different curriculum models. The High/Scope Foundation has documented significant long-term social-behavioral advantages at age 15 for economically disadvantaged children who were involved in preschool curriculum models (the High/Scope model and traditional nursery school) featuring child-initiated activities as compared with economically disadvantaged children involved in the direct instruction model (Schweinhart, Weikart and Larner 1986). Proponents of the direct instruction model report advantages for direct instruction students in a large longitudinal study of a four-year (K-3) Head Start Follow Through project (Gersten and Keating 1986).

Parent Involvement. The fifth component in quality preschool programs is parent involvement. Parent involvement—in parent advisory boards, parent-teacher conferences, family services, and as volunteers and employees—is a hallmark of the Head Start program. The state survey did not directly address parent involvement issues, but we know that parent involvement is included in programs in states that require a comprehensive developmental approach.

The district survey included specific questions about parent involvement. The responses to those questions indicate that nearly all programs offer parent-teacher conferences, about half have parent advisory groups, and an equal number use parent volunteers. Mitchell (1987b) notes that parent advisory bodies are much more likely to be found in Head Start programs and child care programs than in the other program types.

An important factor in both parent involvement and overall program effectiveness is the extent to which programs accommodate working parents. Data from both the state and district surveys indicate that most programs are half-day, a schedule which creates logistical problems for working parents. In fact, the district survey found that about half of the programs reported scheduling parent conferences after working hours. Most of the programs that reported busing children to locations other than home were special education programs. Summer care was reported mostly by child care and special education programs. Summer programs make up only 1.3 percent of the 1,681 programs in the sample.

Early Childhood Program Challenges

What's happening in early childhood programs can be summarized in two words—growth and uncertainty. In the midst of the growth, uncertainty is perhaps the best general descriptor of the current state of early childhood programs. Many critical issues remain to be resolved: what will be the goals, content, and process of programs for both 4- and 5-year-olds; how will we fund, deliver, and determine who attends new programs for 4-year-olds; and how will we ensure quality in our early childhood programs? With so much growth coupled with such great uncertainty in early childhood education today, it is imperative that public school administrators take the broadest possible long-term perspective in defining and addressing programming challenges.

Our first and most important challenge is to focus on the individual needs of the young children we serve. We can provide the resources and opportunities to meet those needs. Specifically, schools can provide children with:

• a comfortable, safe, and stable environment every day, year round, for all of the hours that parents are at work.

• consistent and nurturing care and education.

• the opportunity to be physically active.

• opportunities to explore and meaningfully interact with the world around them.

• opportunities to interact with, learn from, and be appreciated by other children.

• stimulation and support to develop cognitively, socially, emotionally, and physically in their own time and in their own ways.

Now, at the beginning of a tremendous wave of growth in early childhood programs, is the time to say, yes, we can and will focus every program decision on providing optimal services for our children. It is tempting to focus on the many practical and financial constraints we face today, but by concentrating on problems instead of possibilities, we will lose the vision we need to overcome the problems and make the possibilities come true.

Our second challenge is to focus on how learnings in preschool and kindergarten programs can become the foundation for later grades. Instead of designing preschool programs to offset weaknesses in later programs, I propose that right now we begin cooperative planning among preschool, kindergarten, and primary grade teachers and administrators to create coherent curriculums that will progressively support and build on learning and development throughout the early childhood years. Ultimately, we should be aiming for a continuous ungraded curriculum flow from preschool through 3rd grade. Such a structure would push success upward rather than pushing failure downward.

The third major challenge is to broaden our focus outward to involve *all* of the relevant constituents of early childhood programming in planning, supporting, and receiving services now and in the future. Our children are the most important constituents, and right now most of the children in public preschools are disadvantaged. Learning from and along with their more fortunate peers would enhance children's preparation for success in school and later life. To better our programs, we must broaden the student constituency to include all the children of poverty *and* the children of mainstream America.

Mainstream children are not the only constituents who are uninvolved in the majority of preschool programs today. If we open school programs to all 4-year-olds, then we would also have the interest, commitment, and the potential financial and political resources of a larger and more powerful group of parents.

A final unrecognized constituency is the private sector employers who are already spending millions of dollars to help their employees find quality day care and preschool programs. A recent *Fortune* magazine cover story described corporate efforts to meet the problem. According to the article, about 3,000 corporations now provide some kind of child care assistance, a 50 percent increase since 1984 (Chapman 1987). The Bank America Foundation has underwritten a consortium of corporations and government agencies with a $1.1 million budget to make better child care available in several California counties. I believe there is potential for similar cooperation across the nation, and it should be initiated now by state and local education leaders. With the proper focus, planning, and coordinated action, we can have all the resources we need to provide high-quality programs for our young children.

In conclusion, our most important challenges are a matter of focus. We must focus on how we can meet our children's needs. We must look ahead to how we can support and build successful development and learning throughout the early childhood years. And, finally, we must recognize the needs and resources of all our constituents, and work together to create the future we all want.

References

Beach, C. "Silver Spoon-Feeding the Babes of Yuppies." *Insight*, September 14, 1987, 60-61.

Bennett, W.J. "The Role of the Family in the Nurture and Protection of the Young." *American Psychologist* 43, 3 (1987): 246-250.

Bereiter, C., and Englemann, S. *Teaching Disadvantaged Children in the Preschool*. Englewood Cliffs, N.J.: Prentice-Hall, 1966.

Caldwell, B.M. "Day Care and the Public Schools—Natural Allies, Natural Enemies," *Educational Leadership* 44 (February 1986): 34-39.

Center for Education Statistics. *Condition of Education*. Washington, D.C.: U.S. Government Printing Office, 1985.

Chapman, F.S. "Executive Guilt: Who's Taking Care of the Children?" *Fortune*, February 16, 1987, 30-37.

Children's Defense Fund. *A Children's Defense Budget*. Washington, D.C.: Author, 1987.

Committee for Economic Development. *Investing in Our Children*. New York: Author, 1985.

Committee for Economic Development. *Children in Need*. New York: Author, 1987.

Connell, D.R. "The First 30 Years Were the Fairest: Notes from the Kindergarten and Ungraded Primary (K-1-2)." *Young Children* 42, 5 (1987): 30-37.

Day, B. *Early Childhood Education: Creative Learning Activities*. 3rd ed. New York: Macmillan, in press.

Day, B.D., and K.N. Drake. *Early Childhood Education: Curriculum Organization and Classroom Management*. Alexandria, Va.: Association for Supervision and Curriculum Development, 1983.

Day, B.D., and K.N. Drake. "Developmental and Experiential Programs: The Key to Quality Education and Care of Young Children." *Educational Leadership* 44 (November 1986): 25-27.

Educational Research Service. "A Kindergarten Survey." *Principal* 66, 5 (1986): 22-23.

Elkind, D. "Full-Day Kindergarten." *Young Children* 42, 5 (1987): 2.

Futrell, M.H. "Public Schools and Four-Year-Olds: A Teacher's View." *American Psychologist* 42, 3 (1987): 251-253.

Gersten, R., and Keating, T. "Long-Term Benefits From Direct Instruction." *Educational Leadership* 44 (March 1986): 23-31.

Halpern, R. "Major Social and Demographic Trends Affecting Young Families: Implications for Early Childhood Care and Education." *Young Children* 42, 6 (1987): 34-40.

Hill, P.S. "The Function of Kindergarten." *Young Children* 42, 5 (1987): 12-19.

Hohmann, M., B. Banet, and D.P. Weikart. *Young Children in Action: A Manual for Preschool Educators*. Ypsilanti, Mich.: High/Scope Press, 1979.

Leeper, S., R. Witherspoon, and B.D. Day. *Good Schools for Young Children*, 5th ed. New York: Macmillan Publishing Co., 1984.

Lewis, A.C. "Will Uncle Sam Help Mind the Children?" *Phi Delta Kappan* 66 (1985): 459-460.

Marx, F., and M. Seligson. "Draft Notes on States Findings from the Public School Early Childhood Study." Wellesley, Mass.: College Center for Research on Women, 1987.

McCormick, K. "If Early Education Isn't On Your Agenda Now, It Could Be—And Soon." *The American School Board Journal* 172, 6 (1986): 30-34.

Mitchell, A. "Public Schools and Young Children: A Report of the First National Survey of Public School Districts Regarding their Early Childhood Programs." Paper prepared for American Education Research Association Annual Meeting, Washington, D.C., April 1987a.

Mitchell, A. "Young Children in Public Schools: Preliminary Results from a National Survey of Public School Districts and Site Visits in Twelve

States." New York: Bank Street College Center for Children's Policy, 1987b.

Murray, R. "The Kindergarten Dilemma: Half Day, Full Day, or Every Day." *Catalyst* (1987): 18-21.

Morado, C. "Prekindergarten Programs for 4-Year-Olds: State Involvement in Preschool Education." *Young Children* 41, 5 (1986): 69-71.

National Association for the Education of Young Children. *Developmentally Appropriate Practice*. Washington, D.C.: Author, 1986.

Robinson, S.L. "Kindergarten in America: Five Major Trends." *Phi Delta Kappan* 68, 7 (1987): 529-530.

Sava, S.G. "Development, Not Academics." *Young Children* 42, 5 (1987): 15.

Scarr, S., and R.A. Weinberg. "The Early Childhood Enterprise: Care and Education of the Young." *American Psychologist* 41, 10 (1986): 1140-1146.

Schweinhart, L.J., J.L. Koshel, and A. Bridgman. (1987). "Policy Options for Preschool Programs." *Phi Delta Kappan* 68, 3 (1987): 524-529.

Schweinhart, L.J., D.P. Weikart, and M.B. Larner, M.B. "Consequences of Three Preschool Curriculum Models Through Age 15." *Early Childhood Research Quarterly* 1 (1986): 15-45.

Snyder, T.D. "Trends in Education." *Principal* 66, 1 (1986): 8-12.

Uphoff, J.K., and J. Gilmore. (1986). "Pupil Age at School Entrance—How Many Are Ready for Success?" *Young Children* 41, 4 (1986): 11-16.

Zigler, E.F. "Formal Schooling for Four-Year-Olds? No." *American Psychologist* 42, 3 (1987): 254-260.

2
Engaging Children's Minds: The Implications of Research for Early Childhood Education

LILIAN G. KATZ

During the last five or six years, it has become customary to discuss many of the issues surrounding the education of young children in terms of developmental appropriateness (Bredekamp 1987). However, the concept of development itself has generally been used rather vaguely and without definition. This chapter addresses the question "What should young children be doing?" in light of a concept of development and of contemporary research on children's intellectual and social development and learning.

The Concept of Development

Early childhood education has traditionally drawn heavily on studies of human development. Child study and child development as academic specialities have contributed greatly to the field (Green-

An earlier version of this paper is in press in *Early Schooling: The National Debate*, edited by S.L. Kagan and E. Zigler (New Haven, Conn.: Yale University Press).

berg 1987). The study of child development in particular is typically a major component of early childhood teacher preparation.

It is useful to think of the concept of development as having two major dimensions: the normative and the dynamic (Maccoby 1983, Radke-Yarrow 1987). Each of these dimensions has implications for early childhood education.

The Normative Dimension of Development

The most common use of the concept of development draws on the normative dimension, which addresses what most children can and cannot do at a given age or stage. Examples of the normative dimension include what is most frequently observed in children 2-, 3-, 5-, and 9-years-old, and so on. The normative dimension is applied in discussions of such matters as how many words most children know at a particular age or the average age of learning to walk, to understand time, to conserve volume, and so forth. When we say that an activity is developmentally appropriate, speak of grade-level achievement, or apply Gesell-type developmental measures, we are using the normative dimension of the concept of development.

The Dynamic Dimension of Development

The other major dimension of the concept of development is the dynamic one, which has three interrelated aspects. One deals with the sequence in the ways human beings change over time and with experience. This aspect of development addresses the sequences and stages of learnings, the transformations that occur in capabilities from one age to another, and the order in which developments and learnings occur. Thus, some specialists study processes in the transitions from babbling babyhood to becoming a competent speaker of a language by age 4 or 5.

A second aspect of the dynamic dimension is that of delayed impact (Radke-Yarrow 1987). This concerns the way in which early experience may affect later functioning, particularly with respect to affective and personality development. It attends to possible unconscious determinants of mature behavior that may be due to forgotten early experiences.

A third aspect of the dynamic dimension of development is the long-term cumulative effect of repeated or frequent experiences. An experience that might not affect a child's development if it is occasional might be harmful if it occurs often over a long period of time.

A teacher might not worry if a child is occasionally confused by the directions for completing school tasks. But frequent experience with such confusion may have strong negative cumulative effects on the child's self-confidence. Occasional exposure to a horror movie might not affect a child, but frequent and repeated exposures might have long-term deleterious effects in some children.

The three aspects of the dynamic dimension—sequential change, delayed impact, and cumulative effect—remind us to consider children's experiences in the early years in light of their potential long-term consequences. When both the normative and dynamic dimensions of development are taken into account, it seems reasonable to suggest that just because children can do something when they are young does not mean that they should do it. The distinction between what young children *can* do and what they *should* do is especially critical because most of them appear willing, if not eager, to do what is asked of them. They rarely appear to be suffering, and some even enjoy the activities offered. Most young children are eager to please their teachers. But children's willingness and enjoyment are misleading criteria of the value of an activity. After all, young children enjoy junk food, poor television programs, and other experiences generally agreed not to be in their best interest. Enjoyment of these kinds of things can be tolerated on a few occasions, but it is their potentially damaging cumulative effects that concern many adults. Some toddlers are taught to "read" flash cards. Preschool children can perform rote counting up to the hundreds. Many young children willingly fill out worksheets. Young children can, and frequently do, work assiduously to receive tangible rewards like gold stars and colorful stickers and other tokens. The fact they engage in such activities willingly does not imply that they should: It depends upon what the long-term cumulative effects of such experiences might be.

In the light of this definition of the concept of development, the developmental question is not simply "What can children do?" Nor is it "How do they learn?" Children always learn. Learning is a neutral term: Children learn undesirable as well as desirable things; to mistrust as well as to trust, to hurt as well as to help. The critical developmental question for educators is, "What should young children be doing that best serves their development in the long term?" Thus, the questions concerning what young children should be doing must take into account both the normative and dynamic dimensions of development.

Four Categories of Learning

In drawing inferences from research cited below concerning developmentally appropriate programs for young children, I find it helpful to think in terms of four broad types of learning: knowledge, skills, dispositions, and feelings. (This group of four categories of learning is not exhaustive, and more categories could be added; for the purposes of this discussion, the focus is on these four major ones.)

Knowledge during the early childhood period can be broadly defined as information, ideas, stories, facts, concepts, schemes, songs, names, and other such "contents of mind" that make up much of what is to be covered in a curriculum. Although discovery learning has been valued by early childhood educators, there are limits to the kinds and amounts of knowledge that can be discovered by children. A child cannot ask a gerbil what it is called, what family of mammals it belongs to, and why. Children can be helped to acquire knowledge when adults explain, tell them things, and alert them to relevant phenomena.

Skills can be defined as relatively small units of action or behaviors that are easily observed and occur in brief periods (e.g., walking along a balance beam, cutting out a circle, or writing one's name). Mental skills included in this category can be fairly easily inferred from observed behavior that occurs in small units of time, or on a given occasion (such as counting the fingers on a hand). Skills may be learned partly from observation, imitation, trial and error, instruction, directions, and optimum amounts of drill and practice. Lessons and workbooks can be used to aid the acquisition and strengthening of skills.

Dispositions is a category of learning that seems largely neglected, especially by advocates of "back to basics" and other academically oriented programs. Sometimes referred to as attitudes or attitudes of mind, dispositions are difficult to define (Katz and Raths 1985). For present purposes, they are broadly defined as relatively enduring "habits of mind" or characteristic ways of responding to experience across types of situations. Examples of dispositions are curiosity, generosity, avarice, charitability, and quarrelsomeness.

Dispositions are not likely to be learned from lessons, instructions, or lectures. Children are most likely to learn dispositions from observation and emulation of models. The dispositions "picked up" from others are then shaped and strengthened by being appreciated and acknowledged or ignored. If, for example, we wish to strengthen children's dispositions to be curious, it will be necessary to provide opportunities for children to act out their curiosity. We must then convey our appreciation of the disposition with appropriate responses. Of course, not all dispositions are desirable, and some have to be responded to so that they are weakened. Among the dispositions to be strengthened in early childhood are cooperativeness, curiosity, resourcefulness, and the disposition to be absorbed and interested in worthwhile explorations and activities.

Feelings are roughly defined as subjective emotional or affective states. Among the feelings that concern early childhood educators are belonging, self-confidence, and acceptance (Katz 1985). It is not clear which feelings are learned from experience and which are innate responses to classes of stimuli. Contemporary theorizing emphasizes the interactive nature of emotional development. Feelings such as anger, sadness, and frustration are temporary reactions to situations and experiences. But feelings of competence and incompetence in school or acceptance or rejection in the classroom could be said to be learned in that they are the feelings typically aroused in that context.

Educators are not obliged to choose between emphasizing one of these categories of learning over another. Indeed, one of the most challenging and difficult tasks for educators is to design curriculums so that the achievement of goals in all four categories is mutually inclusive and that the acquisition of worthwhile knowledge, useful skills, desirable dispositions, and feelings are all addressed equally.

Some Risks of Academic Pressures on Young Children

Many observers of recent developments in the early childhood programs have expressed alarm over the "push down phenomenon:" namely, the practice of introducing curriculum previously reserved for 1st grade into kindergarten, and sometimes preschool, classes (Egertson 1987). This appears to me to be doing earlier and earlier what we don't do very well later.

The "Damaged Disposition" Hypothesis

We can successfully instruct young children in such reading skills as phonics, for example, but by requiring drill and practice of young children, we risk undermining their dispositions to be readers. The damaged disposition hypothesis, therefore, suggests that the early introduction of academic or basic skills may run counter to the development of children's dispositions to use those skills in the long run (Katz 1985).

Unfortunately, there is no direct empirical test of the damaged disposition hypothesis. But it seems to me to be a reasonable interpretation of some of the results of longitudinal studies (e.g., Karnes et al. 1983, Miller and Bizzell 1983, Schweinhart et al. 1986, Walberg 1984). As we look at the results of such studies, the early pressure on young children to perform academic tasks introduced through direct instruction (e.g., practice in phonics or workbook exercises) appears quite harmless, or even beneficial, in the short term. Furthermore, children do not, at least at first, appear to resist or dislike the exercises. They are often quite enthusiastic about their achievements as well as some of the rewards that come with them.

But as developmentalists we are obliged to take into account the potential long-term cumulative consequences of early experiences, no matter how benign they appear to be the first time they occur. Results from longitudinal studies (Consortium for Longitudinal Studies 1983) suggest that curriculums and teaching methods should be approached so as to optimize the acquisition of knowledge, skills, desirable dispositions, and feelings and so that these are mutually inclusive goals, giving each type of learning equal weight. It is not very useful to have skills if, in the process of acquiring them, the disposition to use them is lost. On the other hand, having the disposition without the requisite skills is also not a desirable educational outcome. The challenge for educators at every level is to help the learner with both the acquisition of skills and the strengthening of desirable dispositions.

Homogeneity of Treatments

Another risk for preschool programs that emphasize academic or basic skills is that they tend to use a single teaching method and curriculum. The relevant principle here is that use of a single teaching or instructional method (a homogeneous treatment) with a group of children of diverse backgrounds and developmental patterns produces heterogeneous outcomes. Needless to say, we want some outcomes of education to be heterogeneous. But it is reasonable to hypothesize that for those outcomes that we wish to be homogeneous, such as all children having the disposition to be readers, the treatment most likely will have to be heterogeneous. It is reasonable to assume that when a single teaching method is used for a diverse group of young children, a significant proportion of them is likely to fail.

It also seems to me a reasonable hypothesis that the younger the children are, the greater the variety of teaching methods should be (Durkin 1980, Nelson and Seidman 1984); although, for reasons of stability and practicality, there are likely to be limits to how varied the teaching methods can be. This hypothesis is derived from the assumption that the younger the group, the less likely they are to have been socialized into a particular and standard way of responding to their environment; and the more likely it is that the children's background experience related to their readiness to learn is unique and idiosyncratic rather than common and shared. Academically focused curriculums typically adopt a single pedagogical method dominated by workbooks, drill, and practice. Even though such approaches often claim to "individualize" instruction, what is typically individualized is the day on which a child completes a task, rather than the task itself. I suspect that very often "time on task" for the children in such programs could be called "time on deadly task." After a year or two of such schooling, the effect on the disposition to learn is likely to be deadening.

Learned Stupidity

Another risk in introducing young children to academic work prematurely is that those children who cannot relate to the content or tasks required are likely to feel incompetent. When the content or tasks of a lesson for college students are difficult to grasp or perform, the student is very likely to fault the instructor. However, in the case of young children, perhaps older ones as well, repeated experiences of being unable to relate to school work are more likely to lead to the self attribution of stupidity, which can be called "learned stupidity." Such children are then very likely to bring their behavior into line with this attribution.

Interaction as a Context for Early Learning

One of the most reliable principles implied by developmental research is that young children's learning is enhanced when the children are engaged in interactive processes (Brown and Campione 1984, Bruner 1985, Glaser 1984, Karmiloff-Smith 1984, Nelson 1985, Rogoff 1983, Wertsch 1985). In addition to learning through trial, error, and observation, young children gain a great deal cognitively and socially by interacting with each other, adults, and their environment.

This trend in research also implies that children's learning is facilitated when they are involved in active rather than passive activities. One of the weaknesses of having conventional academic tasks included in the "pushed down" elementary school curriculum is the resulting reduction in the extent to which children are engaged in interactive processes.

The Development of Communicative Competence

Early childhood is a critical period in the development of communicative competence: namely, competence in self-expression and in understanding others. Contemporary insights into the development of communicative competence in young children indicate that all three basic functions of language (communication, expression, and reasoning) are strengthened when children are engaged in conversation, rather than when they are simply passively exposed to language. Virtually all aspects of communication are most fully developed when children engage in conversations with adults and other children (Wells 1983).

Conversations are a very special type of interaction in which the content of each participant's responses is contingent upon the other's in a sequential string of interactions. It may very well be that the contingency of the responses of adults to children in and of itself has a powerful effect on the development of their intellects. Conversation is more likely to be prolonged when adults make comments to children than when they ask them questions (Blank 1985).

The work of Bruner (1982) and others suggests that conversation is most likely to occur when children are in small groups of three or four, with or without an adult present. Most teachers of young children recognize the difficulty of encouraging conversation during a whole-group session; they expend much effort reminding children that another child is still speaking or that their turn has not yet come. It seems reasonably clear that children are most likely to engage in conversation when something of interest occurs in context (Bruner 1982, Clark and Wade 1983). I watched a kindergarten teacher who was attempting to engage a class of 5-year-old children in a discussion by asking each in turn, "What is your news today?" Each child struggled to find something headline-worthy to report to his or her disinterested squirming classmates. Perhaps some of these children were learning to listen as the teacher intended, but many appeared to be learning to "tune out" their stammering classmates.

The Development of Interest

One of the important dispositions of concern to educators of young children is interest, or the capacity to "lose oneself" in an activity or concern outside of oneself. Interest refers to the capability of becoming deeply enough absorbed in something to pursue it over time, with sufficient commitment to accept the routine as well as novel aspects of work. Sometimes called intrinsic motivation (Morgan 1984), continuing motivation (Maehr 1982), or self-directed learning (Benware and Deci 1984), this disposition appears to be present in the normal human at birth and is affected by a variety of social-psychological processes throughout childhood.

Recent research (Butler and Nisan 1986) has illuminated the effects of different kinds of feedback on learners' interest and intrinsic motivation, or what I refer to as the disposition called interest. Research on the "overjustification effect" suggests that when children are rewarded for tasks in which they had initially shown interest, the reward is followed by loss of interest in the tasks (Deci and Ryan 1985). In such cases, rewards undermine children's interest. The overjustification effect refers to metacognitive processes assumed to be occurring in children's minds, suggesting that children respond to such rewards by saying to themselves, "It must be wrong to like doing x, if I am given a reward for doing it" (Deci and Ryan 1982, 1985). Since this effect applies especially to those activities children originally find interesting, it suggests that teachers should exercise special care not to offer rewards for those activities young children spontaneously enjoy, find attractive, or are easily encouraged to engage in.

A parallel line of research on related processes suggests that when the positive feedback given to children is general in nature, it may serve to increase productivity but not interest (deCharms 1983). General positive feedback includes vague comments on the part of the teacher like "very good" and "well done" or a decorative smiling face or gold star. On the other hand, if the positive feedback is specific rather than general, particularly if it includes information about the competence of the performance, it serves to strengthen interest. The latter is called a "tribute," the former an "inducement." A tribute is associated with increasing interest once the positive feedback becomes unavailable. Academically oriented programs typically emphasize general positive feedback, ostensibly to give children feelings of success and to spur productivity. This strategy appears to work very well to induce young children to keep working at disembedded, decontextualized, and often very trivial tasks. However, the research on the effects of rewards strongly suggests that children may suffer academic burn-out after two or three years of experience with general positive extrinsic rewards.

The Disposition Toward Mastery and Effort

Extensive research by Dweck and her associates (1986, 1987) suggests that the goals teachers set for the activities they provide have significant cumulative effects on children's dispositions toward effort and mastery. Dweck asserts that school tasks can be set in terms of performance goals or learning goals. A teacher sets performance goals by saying, "Today I want to see how good you are at x" or "How many problems can you get right?" or "How well can you do?" The teacher sets learning goals with phrases like, "Today I want to see how much you can learn" or "How much you can find out about x" or "I would like you to experiment and find out how fast these cars roll over different surfaces."

These two conditions arouse different kinds of responses in children that affect their dispositions toward effort and mastery. Under conditions of performance goals, children focus on gaining favorable judgments or avoiding negative ones. Under conditions of learning goals, children seek to increase their understanding or mastery of something new. Dweck defines the mastery disposition as adaptive, accompanied by "challenge seeking and high, effective persistence in the face of obstacles" (1986, p. 1040). She defines the maladaptive disposition as helplessness, manifested by

challenge avoidance, low persistence in the face of difficulty accompanied by negative affect, anxiety and negative self-attributions with respect to ability. Furthermore, the evidence indicates that the adaptive and maladaptive dispositions are independent of actual intellectual ability (p. 1042).

A variety of research studies (Dweck 1986, 1987) on these two types of goals indicate that they produce different effects on children's concerns as they address the tasks assigned. Under performance goals, children show concern about their ability. Children who are confident about their abilities may accept a task eagerly, though a few will worry that they won't measure up to their high reputations. Others tend to engage in defensive withdrawal from the task in order to avoid expected negative judgments of their ability. Performance goals "promote defensive strategies that can interfere with challenge seeking" (Dweck 1986, p. 1043). Dweck's experiments revealed that when faced with learning goals, children chose challenging tasks regardless of whether they believed themselves to have high or low ability; they also were not reluctant to display their ignorance. They tended to think more about the required skills and the interest of the topic and were less oriented internally toward their own ability and how they might look to others.

In lessons oriented toward performance goals, children who do not succeed tend to attribute their failure to their lack of ability (Dweck 1986, 1987). This kind of self-attribution usually leads to anxiety, which may interfere with their performance and ultimately to withholding effort. A few children even become overwhelmed with worry about goal attainment. During learning-goal assignments, children perceive obstacles and difficulties as cues to increase their effort, to analyze and vary their strategies, and thus to improve their work. As Dweck points out, "the more children focus on learning or progress, the greater the likelihood of maintaining effective strategies (or improving their strategies) under difficulty or failure" (1986, p. 1044).

The two types of task goals give rise to different sources of satisfaction. Under the performance goals condition, children perceive an opportunity to display their abilities, take pride in them if they are able, or experience embarrassment and shame when they fail. Experience with performance goals leads children to the view that effort indicates low ability. They then engage in attempts to disguise or deny the application of real effort, fearing that it will reveal that they have little ability. Children with a strong performance orientation derive satisfaction in outshining others and in the failure of others and enjoy a competitive reward structure. In the case of learning goals, children gain enjoyment and satisfaction from the effort involved as well as from the mastery achieved. Learning-oriented children have also been found to be more magnanimous toward their peers in noncompetitive situations (Dweck 1986). Dweck's research indicates also that under the learning goals condition there is greater transfer of learning and more active attempts to apply what has been learned to novel problems. Contrary to common sense, "continued success on personally easy tasks with a performance goal . . . is ineffective in producing stable confidence, challenge seeking and persistence" (Dweck 1986, p. 1046).

The research summarized above suggests that the disposition sometimes called "learning to learn," mastery, challenge seeking, or the tendency to maintain effort in the face of difficulties can be threatened by *excessive* emphasis on skilled performances in academically oriented curriculums. Dweck notes that emphasis on performance "may well create the very conditions that have been found to undermine intrinsic interest" (1986, p. 1042).

As suggested elsewhere (Katz 1977), curriculums and teaching methods that attempt to provide children with constant amusement, fun, and excitement also risk undermining the development of children's disposition for interest. Thus, the teacher's role in strengthening children's dispositions to be interested in relevant and worthwhile phenomena is a complex and highly critical one. Furthermore, since the disposition to lose oneself in an activity may be threatened by frequent interruptions, teachers need to build flexibility into the time they allocate for various activities in order to avoid fragmenting them.

Social Competence

Although definitions of social competence vary on some of the details, they generally include the capacity to initiate, develop, and maintain satisfying relationships with others, especially peers. Social competence does not require children to be social butterflies. It is not a source of concern if children choose to work or play alone, as long as they are also capable of interacting productively and successfully with others when desired or when appropriate.

However, contemporary research indicates that children who have not acquired minimal social competence by the age of about six are more likely to become school dropouts (Gottman 1983, Parker and Asher 1987). They will also be at significant risk in young adulthood in terms of mental health, marital adjustment, and other aspects of social life in which interpersonal competence is required (Parker and Asher 1986, 1987).

The acquisition of social competence involves many complex processes beginning in early infancy. It should be noted that inappropriate, as well as appropriate, social responses are learned through interaction. Weaknesses in social competence may be intensified during such interactions unless adults help children alter maladaptive patterns. In the preschool period, inadequate peer-interactive skills are unlikely to be improved through formal instruction or even coaching; rather, they can be modified by the intervention of a knowledgeable teacher (see Katz 1984). Fortunately, a range of techniques that teachers can use to foster the development of social competence is now available (Burton 1987, Katz 1984).

It is useful to think of social competence as having the characteristics of a recursive cycle. The principle of the recursive cycle is that once an individual has a given behavior or characteristic, reactions to him or her tend to increase the chances that he or she will display more of that behavior or characteristic. For example, children who are likable, attractive, and friendly tend to elicit positive responses in others fairly easily, and because they receive such positive responses, they become more likable, attractive, and friendly. Similarly, children who are unattractive, unfriendly, and difficult to like tend to be avoided or rejected by others. In response to this avoidance and rejection, they tend to behave in ways that make them even more unattractive. This, in turn, increases the likelihood that they will more often be avoided or rejected, and the cycle becomes well-established. This general principle can be applied to many kinds of behavior and learning, but especially to social behaviors (Patterson 1986).

The principle of the recursive cycle implies that young children should be engaged in interactive processes, especially in the company of teachers who have specialized training and competencies in helping young children maximize the educational potential of interaction (Katz 1986). Unfortunately, young children by themselves cannot break a negative cycle. Even for adults, breaking a dysfunctional cycle alone is very difficult. Young children have virtually no capacity to understand the cause of their social difficulties and make the necessary adjustments; adults must intervene by teaching young children more productive peer interactive patterns during ongoing social interactions.

Experience suggests that if we respond to children's needs for help in the development of their social competence in the early years, we can do a great deal to get them on a positive cycle and relieve them of much anguish that inevitably accompanies social difficulties in childhood. If we wait until children are 9 or 10 years old and making life difficult for themselves or for others, we may need substantial resources from a mental health agency to intervene, and still may be too late. These recent insights from research (Parker and Asher 1986) on children's social competence suggest that preschool teachers' concern with social development is well placed and should be given as much weight in planning and teaching as is children's intellectual development.

Some Curriculum Options

Many people within and without the field of early childhood education think that the choice for curriculum is to have *either* an academic *or* a socialization focus. Some of the risks of introducing academic tasks to young children have already been suggested. But the alternative to overemphasis on academic work is not simply to provide spontaneous play (though all children up to about 7 or 8 years of age can probably benefit from it). Rather, the data (Consortium on Longitudinal Studies 1983) on children's learning seem to suggest that what is required in preschool and kindergarten is an intellectually oriented approach in which children interact in small groups as they work together on a variety of projects that help them make sense of their own experience.

Children's dispositions toward sustained involvement and interest can be strengthened when they are encouraged to engage in projects that call for effort and involvement over time and provide contexts for extension, elaboration, and continuation of work and play (Rosenfield et al. 1980). These projects should also strengthen their dispositions to observe, experiment, inquire, and reconstruct aspects of their environment.

In addition to the insights drawn from the aforementioned research on specific aspects of development, research on the impacts of different kinds of early childhood curriculums supports the view that young children should be in preschool and kindergarten programs that provide opportunities for interaction, active rather than passive activities, and ample opportunities to initiate activities that interest them (Fry and Addington 1984, Koester and Farley 1982). The benefits of informal, interactive teaching methods are especially striking in the long term and notably discouraging in the short term (Miller and Bizzell 1983, Schweinhart et al. 1986). According to Walberg (1984), a synthesis of 153 studies of open education, including 90 dissertations, indicates that

the average effect [size for open education] was near zero for achievement, focus of control, self-concept, and anxiety (which suggests no difference between open and control classes on these criteria); about .2 for adjustment, attitude toward schools and teachers, curiosity, and general mental ability; and about a moderate .3 for cooperativeness, creativity, and independence.

Thus students in open classes do no worse in standardized achievement and slightly to moderately better on several outcomes that educators, parents and students hold to be of great value." (1984, p. 25).

In sum, insights derived from developmental and related curriculums research supports the view that a significant proportion of the time children spend in preschool and kindergarten classes should be allocated to the kind of project or unit work characteristic of pedagogical methods that are intellectually oriented and informal. This classroom approach was known in the 1960s as open education, the integrated day, or informal methods.

It is reasonable to assume that many young children can benefit from some work on academic tasks and from opportunities to engage in spontaneous play. However, neither of these two kinds of activities is sufficient for young minds to grow on. The research reviewed above suggests to me that intellectual development can be greatly enhanced by engaging children in work on the kinds of group projects described briefly below.

The Value of Project Work for Young Children

The project approach is a particularly promising strategy for fostering children's interactions as suggested by contemporary research (Katz and Chard in press). A project is a group undertaking, usually around a particular theme or topic. A project involves a variety of kinds of work over a period of several days or weeks.

Types of projects. There are three basic types of projects, though some are combinations of two or more. During the preschool period, the most common type of project consists of reconstructing environmental aspects within the preschool or primary school setting. Another type of project consists of investigating aspects of the environment and includes development of various ways to report the findings of the investigations to classmates. A third type consists largely of observing aspects of the environment and preparing ways to present or report what was learned from the observations to others in the class. Certainly many projects may be various mixtures of the three basic types.

A topic or theme for a project, depending in part on the ages of the children, may be introduced by the teacher or children or evolve from discussions they have together. There may or may not be a project leader who coordinates the activities of the group. On some occasions, the membership of the project group may fluctuate; at other times, it may be beneficial to require stability in group membership or to encourage the members to carry their part of a project through to completion.

Project phases. Projects usually have three rough phases that are likely to blend into each other. First is a planning phase during which children and staff members discuss the elements of the project, develop plans and procedures for obtaining the materials, build the elements, or carry out the investigations and observations. This phase would also include discussions about what information to obtain during field trips or site visits and provide ample opportunities for rich discussion and for children to display and generate interest in the project.

A second phase consists of constructing or building the parts of the project, gathering information or making observations, or making pictures so others in the class can share what has been learned. A third phase includes role playing, or taking the roles appropriate to the various elements of the project. During this period, extensions and elaborations of the project may be undertaken. Almost any aspect of the environment can become the focus of a project. Many opportunities for cooperative social interaction occur in all three phases of a project.

Among the examples of the project approach are two kindergarten classes I know of in different parts of the country that undertook detailed studies of their school bus. In one of the classes, one small group studied the driving mechanism, including the motor and gear shifts, brakes, accelerator, and steering wheel. Another group examined the variety of lights inside and outside the bus. It was noted by some of the children that some lights are for signals, others are to give a warning, and others, of course, are to light the way ahead as well as inside. Some lights were red, others yellow, or white; some flashed on and off, and some were merely reflectors. Other children in the class studied the gauges and dials in the bus and what kinds of information they yield. Another group took measurements of the width of the bus, counted the number of seats and wheels, and learned something about air pressure in the tires. A few children examined the inside and outside rearview mirrors.

It is not difficult to imagine the kind of vocabulary building that can accompany such a study: terms like ignition, emergency door, fuel, dial, gauge, air pressure, accelerator, rearview mirror, and gears. Those children able to do so copied down all the "writing" they could find on the bus and used it for vocabulary, writing, and reading studies in the classroom. The door of the school bus opened and closed with a lever, and the children made several flawed attempts to reproduce this feature of the bus in the one they built in their classroom before they got it right. Their efforts involved much genuine problem-solving

Similar activities were undertaken by another kindergarten class. They constructed a bus constructed of heavy-duty cardboard and old packing cases. A special large box containing a motor with a collection of cardboard parts was featured on the front of it. Windshield wipers and reflector lights were a big feature of the bus, and a large mass of cotton representing the exhaust was prominently placed at the rear. The construction of the bus extended over a period of nearly two months as children continued to add details and repair the parts that broke down with the heavy use they received during dramatic play.

Virtually all aspects of the work undertaken by the children in this project lent themselves to art work, including drawing, painting, and making paper, plasticene, or wooden models. Aspects of the basic skills also came into play as children counted seats, measured the length and width of the bus, and read and reproduced the writing inside and outside the bus. There is no special virtue to studying a school bus in the sense that some important test will ever examine the knowledge the children gained from the project. What is important is that the bus is part of the children's own daily environment and that they learned a lot about it: the correct names of various parts of it, a simple understanding of how it works, and what features of it contribute to their safety. The project provided a context in which children's dispositions to observe, inquire and become interested and involved in a sustained group effort could be strengthened.

In a project of this type, the teacher alerts children to a wide range of potentially interesting aspects of the topic that will take several days or even weeks of continuous probing and exploring. The use of adults other than just teachers as source of potentially valuable information can be launched through this kind of project. Students can ask questions of adults such as the bus driver and perhaps a mechanic, or they can look up facts in reference books of appropriate levels of difficulty. The fact that the children are expected to tell and explain what they have learned to their own classmates is likely to encourage persistence in attaining information and reaching for adequate understanding (Benware and Deci 1984). Furthermore, for many of the children in the class, the project is likely to strengthen their dispositions to observe other vehicles more closely than they had before, perhaps making useful comparisons and reporting them to their classmates from time to time.

In sum, the project approach can be valuable for young children because it can engage their minds and thereby address their intellects. It can strengthen a variety of important dispositions, provide rich content for conversation, and a context for peer interaction in which cooperative effort makes sense. Projects are also culturally relevant in that they stem from the children's own interests and environments. Finally, it should not be overlooked that another important virtue of the project approach is that it can make teaching interesting—something very unlikely to be typical of programs that overemphasize the formal academic approaches to early childhood education. The inclusion of project work in the curriculum is consistent with the intention to engage young children's minds in improving their understandings of relevant phenomena in their environment, and to provide a context in which the development and application of their social competencies are strongly encouraged. Both intellectual and social development can be well served by the project approach.

I have suggested that the project approach is not only developmentally appropriate, it is also culturally appropriate. And since it can also make teaching interesting, it provides a context in which children can observe adults intellectually engaged and interested in what they are doing. As I see it, we are not caught between either an academic or socialization focus. I do not wish to suggest that either focus should be dropped from the early childhood curriculum. The main argument of this chapter is that part of the curriculum should involve children in the kinds of activities that engage and challenge their minds more fully than either academic or play activities typically do. As I see it, contemporary research on young children's learning implies that the younger they are, the larger the proportion of their time should be allocated to the kind of informal project work proposed in this chapter.

References

Benware, C.A., and E.L. Deci. "Quality of Learning with an Active versus Passive Motivational Set." *American Educational Research Journal* 211, 4 (1984): 755-765.

Blank, M. "Classroom Discourse: The Neglected Topic of the Topic." In *Helping Communication in Early Education*, edited by M.M. Clark. Education Review Occasional Publications No. 11, 1985.

Bredekamp, Sue. *Developmentally Appropriate Practice in Early Childhood Programs Serving Children from Birth through Age 8*. Washington, D.C.: National Association for the Education of Young Children, 1987.

Brown, A.L., and J.C. Campione. "Three Faces of Transfer: Implications for Early Competence Individual Differences, and Instruction." In *Advances in Developmental Psychology*, edited by M.E. Lamb, A.L. Brown, and B. Rogoff. Vol. 3. Hillsdale, N.J.: Lawrence Erlbaum Associates, 1984.

Bruner, J. *Under Five in Britain*. Vol. 1. Oxford Preschool Research Project. Ypsilanti, Mich.: High/Scope Foundation, 1982.

Bruner, J. "Vygotsky: A Historical and Conceptual Perspective." In *Culture, Communication and Cognition. Vygotskian Perspectives*, edited by J. Wertsch. Cambridge: Cambridge University Press, 1985.

Burton, C.B. "Problems in Children's Peer Relations: A Broadening Perspective." In *Current Topics in Early Childhood Education*, edited by L.G. Katz. Vol 7. Norwood, N.J.: Ablex, 1987.

Butler, Ruth, and Mortecai Nisan. "Affects of No Feedback, Task-Related Comments, and Grades on Intrinsic Motivation and Performance." *Journal of Educational Psychology* 78, 3 (June 1986): 210-216.

Clark, M.M., and B. Wade. "Early Childhood Education." *Educational Review* 35, 2 (1983): Special Issue (15).

Consortium for Longitudinal Studies. *As the Twig is Bent*. Hillsdale, N.J.: Erlbaum, 1983.

deCharms, R. "Intrinsic Motivation, Peer Tutoring, and Cooperative Learning: Practical Maxims." In *Teacher and Student Perceptions: Implications for Learning*, edited by J.M. Levine and M.C. Want. Hillsdale, N.J.: Erlbaum, 1983.

Deci, E.L., and R.M. Ryan. "Curiosity and Self-Directed Learning." In *Current Topics in Early Childhood Education*, edited by L.G. Katz. Vol. 4. Norwood, N.J.: Ablex, 1982.

Deci, E., and R. Ryan. *Intrinsic Motivation and Self Determination*. N.Y.: Plenum Press, 1985.

Durkin, D. "Is Kindergarten Reading Instruction Really Desirable?" *Ferguson Lectures in Education*. Evanston, Ill.: National College of Education, 1980.

Dweck, C.S. "Motivational Processes Affecting Learning." *American Psychologist*. 41, 10 (1986): 1040-1048.

Fry, P.S., and J. Addington. "Comparison of Social Problem Solving of Children from Open and Traditional Classrooms: A Two-Year Longitudinal Study." *Journal of Educational Psychology* 76, 1 (1984): 318-329.

Glaser, R. "Education and Thinking: The Role of Knowledge." *American Psychologist* 39, 2 (1984): 93-104.

Gottman, J.M. "How Children Become Friends." *Monographs of the Society for Research in Child Development* 48, 3 (1983): Serial No. 201.

Greenberg, P. "Lucy Sprague Mitchell: A Major Missing Link Between Early Childhood Education in the 1980s and Progressive Education in the 1890s–1930s." *Young Children* 42, 5 (1987): 70-84.

Karmiloff-Smith, A. "Children's Problem Solving." In *Advances in Develop-*

mental Psychology, edited by M. Lamb, A. Brown, and B. Rogoff. Vol. 3. Hillsdale, N.J.: Lawrence Erlbaum Associates, 1984.

Karnes M.B., A.M. Schwedel, and M.B. Williams. "A Comparison of Five Approaches for Educating Young Children from Low-Income Homes." In *As the Twig is Bent . . . Lasting Effects of Preschool Programs*, edited by the Consortium for Longitudinal Studies. Hillsdale, N.J.: Lawrence Erlbaum Associates, 1983.

Katz, L.G. "Education or Excitement." In *Talks with Teachers*, edited by L.G. Katz. Washington, DC: National Association for the Education of Young Children, 1977.

Katz, L.G. "The Professional Preschool Teacher." In *More Talks with Teachers*, edited by L.G. Katz. Urbana, Ill.: ERIC Clearinghouse on Elementary and Early Childhood Education, 1984.

Katz, L.G. "Dispositions in Early Childhood Education." *ERIC/EECE Bulletin* 18, 2 (1985).

Katz, L.G. "Current Perspectives on Child Development." Council for Research in Music Education Bulletin No. 86:1-9, 1986.

Katz, L.G. "The Professional Early Childhood Teacher." *Young Children*, July 1984, 3-9.

Katz, L.G., and J.D. Raths. "Dispositions as Goals for Teacher Education." *Teaching and Teacher Education* 1, 4 (1985): 301-307.

Katz, L.G., and S.C. Chard. *Engaging the Minds of Young Children: The Project Approach*. Norwood, N.J.: Ablex, in press

Koester, L.S., and F. Farley. "Psychophysical Characteristics and School Performance of Children in Open and Traditional Classrooms." *Journal of Educational Psychology* 74, 2 (1982): 254-263.

Maccoby, E.E. "Socialization and Developmental Change." *Child Development* 55, 2 (1984): 317-328.

Maehr, M.L. *Motivational Factors in School Achievement.* ED 227 095, 1982.

Miller, Louise B., and Rondeal P. Bizzell. "Long-term Effects of Four Preschool Programs: Sixth, Seventh, and Eighth Grades." *Child Development* 54 (June 1983): 727-41.

Morgan, M. "Reward-Induced Decrements and Increments in Instrinsic Motivation." *Review of Education Research* 54, 1 (1984): 5-30.

Nelson, K. *Making Sense: The Acquisition of Shared Meaning.* N.Y.: Academic Press, 1985.

Nelson, K., and S. Seidman. "Playing with Scripts." In *Symbolic Play. The Development of Social Understanding*, edited by I. Bretherton. N.Y.: Academic Press, 1984.

Parker, J., and S. Asher. "Predicting Later Outcomes from Peer Rejection: Studies of School Drop Out, Delinquency and Adult Psychopathology." Paper presented at the annual conference of the American Educational Research Association, San Francisco, March 1986.

Parker, Jeffrey G., and Steven R. Asher. "Peer Relations and Later Preschool Adjustment: Are Low Accepted Children At Risk?" *Psychological Bulletin* 102, 3 (1987).

Patterson, G. R. "Performance Models for Antisocial Boys." *American Psychologist* 41, 4 (1986): 432-444.

Radke-Yarrow, M. "A Developmental and Contextual Analysis of Continuity." A paper presented at the biennial conference of the Society for Research in Child Development, Baltimore, April 1987.

Rogoff, B. "Integrating Context and Cognitive Development." In *Advances in Developmental Psychology*, edited by M.E. Lamb and A.L. Brown. Vol. 2. Hillsdale, N.J.: Lawrence Erlbaum Associates, 1983.

Rosenfield, D., R. Folger, and H.F. Adelman. "When Rewards Reflect Competence: A Qualification of Overjustification Effect." *Journal of Personality and Social Psychology* 39, 3 (1980): 368-376.

Schweinhart, L.J., D.P. Weikart, and M.B. Larner. "Consequences of Three Preschool Curriculum Models through Age 15." *Early Childhood Research Quarterly* 1, 1 (1986): 15-46.

Walberg, H. "Improving the Productivity of Americans' Schools." *Educational Leadership* 41, 8 (1984): 19-30.

Wells, G. "Talking with Children: The Complementary Roles of Parents and Teachers." In *Early Childhood Development and Education*, edited by M. Donaldson, R. Grieve, and C. Pratt. London: The Guilford Press, 1983.

Wertsch, J. *Vygotsky and the Social Formation of the Mind*. Cambridge, Mass.: Harvard University Press, 1985.

3
The Resistance to Developmentally Appropriate Educational Practice with Young Children: The Real Issue

DAVID ELKIND

Although the foundations of early childhood education were laid down more than a century ago, by Froebel and Montessori, this domain of education remains little understood and appreciated today. Many parents and educators fail to recognize the enormous amount of experience that infants and young children have to reconstruct and how they go about doing it. Because of this failure, the promise of early childhood education—to provide children with a solid data base essential for later learning, a strong sense of self-esteem, an excitement and curiosity about learning, and an enthusiasm for schooling—has yet to be realized for many children. This promise can only be fulfilled when the environment, materials, and teaching practices employed with young children are appropriate to their levels of understanding and to their unique modes of learning.

It seems reasonable to ask why the accumulation of theory, research, and teaching experience in favor of instructing children at their level of intellectual, social, and physical maturity has not been accompanied by an equally broad acceptance of developmentally appropriate education for young children. Many parents and educators are still convinced that young children should be taught as if they were miniature 1st or 2nd graders, with workbooks, homework, tests, and grades.

Why is it that people have so much difficulty appreciating the psychology of the young child and accepting developmentally appropriate teaching practices? Perhaps the answer can be understood in the context of a broader question: What world view does the advocacy of developmentally appropriate curriculums represent, and with what world view does it conflict? Put differently, we are confronted with the kind of conflict between opposed world views that Kuhn (1970) described in his classic work, *The Structure of Scientific Revolutions*.

From this point of view, developmentally appropriate curriculums and teaching practices contradict much of the pedagogy in today's schools. This resistance to such developmentally appropriate practice at the early childhood level is but a fraction of the resistance its advocates encounter at higher grade levels. Thus, any acceptance of developmentally appropriate practice at the early childhood level can be seen as an opening wedge to its introduction at all age levels.

Still, the resistance to such a change is perplexing. Kuhn points out that science does not grow by gradual accretion but by revolution. The science of any historical period is part of a closely woven set of social, cultural, economic, and scientific concepts and values that Kuhn calls a paradigm. New ideas threaten this paradigm until their benefits outweigh those of the prevailing paradigm. The new fabric of ideas and values then replaces what went before. There has been a revolution, a paradigm shift, in the sense that the new ideas and values often contradict, rather than build upon, those of the previous paradigm.

In effect, then, developmentally appropriate practice at the early childhood level is only a small part of a much larger paradigm that challenges and contradicts the prevailing paradigm in education. And because this paradigm is so well entrenched, so encrusted with existing habits of thought and practice, so supportive of a comfortable way of life for many people, any challenge to it must be resisted. The resistance takes many forms that range from devaluing those who advocate the new paradigm to accepting and sabotaging it at the same time.

A full discussion of the existing paradigm is beyond the scope of this chapter, but a simple example will help to illustrate how tightly woven it is with existing values and why any challenge to it will be strongly resisted.

In many communities around the country, elementary school children are rotated. In some schools, even 1st graders go to different rooms for reading, math, and social studies. The rationale is that this permits the teacher to specialize and thus be more effective than a generalist might be. Even if we accept this rationale, where is it written that the children must rotate?

From the point of view of energy expenditure and the most efficient use of children's time in school, it would make more sense for teachers to rotate from classroom to classroom. Since it is more convenient for teachers to have their own rooms, desks, and materials in one place, rotation, then, is for the benefit of teachers regardless of whether it is the best pedagogical arrangement for children. It is interesting how the paradigm shields contradictory information. There has been a lot of discussion of late about the values of Japanese education, much of it describing how hard parents work to help their children with their homework and so on. Yet we Americans fail to note an important part of the Japanese education practice: In Japanese schools, even at the high school level, the teachers rotate.

The existing paradigm is extraordinarily complex and tied up in so many ways with the education establishment that it would take a book to describe. Nonetheless, it appears that the existing paradigm has been built upon a "kernel idea." It is this kernel idea that the new paradigm has challenged. And if that foundation kernel were destroyed, the whole edifice would fall. It seems worthwhile, then, to describe this kernel idea and the new idea that challenges it.

The Existing Paradigm

Despite many denials, the paradigm that dominates contemporary American education is behavioral. At the heart of the behavioral paradigm is the assumption that only those entities that can be measured are of value psychologically and, by extension, educationally. Stimuli and responses, test questions, and answers are all that are measurable and, therefore, all that are valuable from a behavioral point of view. B.F. Skinner (1971) is perhaps among the few psychologists who still hold explicitly to this view. Nonetheless, the behavioral view is still implicit in educational settings where testing drives the curriculum and is the final arbiter in decisions about individual retention and advancement.

Implicit in this orientation is the concept of the child as a more or less empty bottle that gets filled up with many facts and skills at each grade level. Moreover, children are taught according to a set of learning principles that have been demonstrated experimentally, and can be employed in the classroom. The efficacy of these principles can be measured by standardized tests. In addition, classroom management can also be accomplished using a set of well-defined behavioral principles. With such an approach one does not have to think about children thinking, only about how best to present the material to get the most correct responses and the highest test scores. While this is an exaggeration, and certainly far from true for all schools and teachers, it portrays the philosophy that underlies a great deal of educational practice in this country.

A corollary belief to the conviction that anything of value in psychology or education is measurable is that one can arrive at the structure of knowledge and the steps of the learning process by logical analysis and reflection. Perhaps no other concept reflects this belief more clearly than that of "behavioral objectives." How are such objectives arrived at? In most cases it happens as follows: An individual, or a group of individuals, sits down and reflects upon what does or should go on in the classroom. The objectives are defined and become goals of instruction. Bloom's (1974) steps in mastery learning are a more elaborate example of this belief in our ability to arrive at how children learn by reflection.

This corollary also presupposes that all that is worth knowing or measuring is observable, and that reflection and logical analysis are simply alternative ways of observing—mental observation, if you will. Moreover, one can always test the results of reflection and analysis to ensure that observations made in this way are correct. Unfortunately, this does not happen, and once the results of reflection and analysis are built into a curriculum, they are apt to remain there indefinitely, whether or not they work in the classroom. The concept of number lines, for example, is found in many math workbooks for 2nd graders despite the fact that few 2nd graders can grasp the notion of infinity implicit in the number line.

This example touches upon a powerful reinforcer of resistance to a new paradigm. The publishers of curriculum materials have a vested interest in the prevailing paradigm. It supports, after all, a multimillion dollar business. Also, curriculum publishers are conservative and operate to preserve the status quo. If one company has a number line in a 2nd grade workbook, then all companies will have number lines in their math books for the 2nd grade in order to compete. It really doesn't matter that the workbook may not make much sense to the children it is supposed to instruct. And often, after a teacher has organized material so it will matter, a new edition of the workbook appears that is every bit as inappropriate as the one that preceded it.

At the heart of the prevailing paradigm, then, is the idea that anything worth teaching is measurable and observable either directly or indirectly through reflection or logical analysis. There is no need, therefore, to know anything about child development or to heed the experience of teachers in the classroom.

The New Paradigm

Although a full discussion of the new paradigm, spearheaded by the work of Jean Piaget (1950), is beyond the scope of this chapter, we can look at its kernel ideas upon which the rest of the paradigm is constructed. At the heart of the new paradigm is the construct of the intellective unconscious, the idea that much of our thinking and reasoning goes on outside of our conscious awareness and that we cannot get at it by reflection or logical analysis.

The contradiction between the kernel ideas at the heart of the two paradigms is now very clear. For the behavioral paradigm, only that which can be observed and measured has psychological or educational value. The intellective unconscious which, by definition, is neither observable nor measurable, clearly falls outside the domain of acceptable psychological and educational phenomena. Yet it is at the heart of the new paradigm and forms the foundation for developmentally appropriate curriculum. Given the centrality of this concept, we need to look at the evidence for it.

In the course of his investigations into the mental development of children, Piaget found that some mental processes became unconscious as they became entrenched and automatized. They became unconscious in the sense that they were no longer directly accessible to reflection. How mental processes get relegated to the intellective unconscious is perhaps most easily observed in the changes in awareness that accompany a child's discovery of conservation.

In the Piagetian lexicon, conservation has to do with the child's construction of a concept (object, space, time, number, mass, weight, or volume) that enables the child to go beyond perceptual impressions and to recognize permanence despite apparent change or difference. A child who judges six pennies close together as the same number as six pennies spread apart has demonstrated conservation. The concept of number, of the sameness of six elements regardless of their configuration, has won out over the perceptual impression of difference. A true test of conservation always presents the child with a conflict between judgments based on reason and those based on perception.

Of particular interest here are the changes in the child's awareness that accompany the changes in judgment. When a 4-year-old is shown the conservation of liquid task, the child says that the amount of liquid poured from a low, wide container into a tall, narrow container is "more" than the same amount of liquid in the first container because the level of the liquid is higher in the tall container than in the low one. At this stage, the child is clearly aware of the basis for choice.

However, when this same child is tested at the age of seven, a very different picture emerges. The child is amused when questioned about whether the amount of liquid in the tall, narrow container has more or less liquid than that in the low, wide container. The child replies that the two amounts are the same because, "You didn't add anything or take anything away," or that "What the tall one gained in height it lost in width." These replies, like those of the younger child, reflect the older child's awareness of the basis for judgment.

But we need to examine the situation a little more closely. The young child, no less than the older child, knew that nothing had been added or taken away. Why does this information become relevant at one age and not at another? To understand this difference we have to recognize that the equality of the liquids in a tall, narrow and a low, wide container cannot be discovered by observation. In fact, the comparison of the liquid in a tall, narrow container with that in a low, wide container presents an illusion of inequality. Only when looking at the two quantities in relation to the transformation can the child overcome the illusion and discover the equality. Even then, the transformation has to be inserted within a logical argument in order for the child to deduce conservation.

In effect the child who attains conservation reasons as follows:

A = B The quantities in two low, wide containers are the same.

A [=] A' The quantity of liquid in the low container remains the same when poured into the tall, narrow container A'.

∴ A' = B The quantity of liquid in the low, wide container is the same as that in the tall, narrow container.

Although the older child's judgment is correct and based on a sound logical argument, it is explained on the basis of perception. Whether the child says "you didn't add anything, or take anything away" or "the liquid got taller but thinner so it is the same," the child provides a perceptual explanation for a logical deduction. In effect, the child is not aware of having passed from making judgments on the basis of perception to making judgments on the basis of reason.

The older child, therefore, is less aware than the younger child of the mental processes that underlie his or her judgment. And the same is true for the affective unconscious. Young children are more aware of their affective unconscious than they will be as they grow older. This is evident in children's dreams, which are often direct wish fulfillments with little elaboration by what Freud (1938) called the "dream work." A young child who wishes for an ice cream cone simply dreams of an ice cream cone. For older children and adults, the object of the wish wears a symbolic disguise. In short, as we mature, we become increasingly less aware of the working of both our affective and our intellective unconscious.

This development away from awareness of our unconscious processing is very adaptive. Our mental processes become increasingly complex as our reasoning matures and our fund of information, skills, and values multiplies. It would be tedious to be fully aware of the history and intricate reasoning that underlies our grasp of a particular instance of causality. Our feelings, emotions, and motives also become more complex and intricate with maturity. And while it might be instructive to understand why we are attracted to one person rather than another, getting at that understanding might take years of analysis.

This distancing from our unconscious processing is paralleled in what happens when we become proficient in a motor skill, such as typing or playing the piano, which has a complex intellectual substructure. Once we have mastered these skills, they become automatized to the extent that any fleeting awareness of our discrete actions interferes with our performance. In the same way, being aware of all the automatized emotional and cognitive processes that underlie making a particular decision would only impair the effective making of that decision. In short, the older we get, the more automatized and unconscious are the cognitive processes that underlie our thought and behavior.

There is another process that contributes to our inability to fully appreciate the role of the intellective unconscious in our everyday thought and behavior. It is the process of externalization. As we saw in the case of the older child who has attained conservation, once the child is convinced that the quantities remain the same despite a change in their appearance, the child also believes that it is a perceptual given. That is to say, we tend to attribute the result of the intellective unconscious to perception impression rather than to unconscious reasoning.

Indeed, the phenomenon of externalization makes it difficult for all adults to arrive at an understanding of the intellective unconscious without guidance. For example, when we attempt to explain our thoughts and behavior, we often refer to external, perceptual features rather than to internal, cognitive precesses. Many gifted and talented teachers, like many gifted and talented therapists, are really incapable of explaining in depth what it is they do and how they achieve their wondrous effects. When pressed for an answer, they often give a perceptual or behavioral explanation: "I guess I give them a lot of freedom to choose" or "I suppose I am very patient." The inability of such individuals to communicate their talents is strong evidence of the presence of the intellective unconscious and its inaccessibility to direct reflection.

The Ongoing Paradigm Battle

The current battle for developmentally appropriate curriculums in the schools can thus be seen in the context of an ongoing larger battle between two opposed paradigms regarding the nature of human learning and how we access that learning. Although there is clearly much wrong with the existing paradigm, and new indictments of the school continue to appear, current reform movements have not really attempted to go beyond the existing system. Extending the school day or year, merit pay, voucher systems, and revised curriculums support the established paradigm. Even the cooperative learning movement still accepts the premise that all valuable knowledge and teaching is directly measurable and observable.

Fortunately, education does not exist in a vacuum. The rapid growth of cognitive science is building a new data base with respect to thinking and learning that does not hold direct measurability and observability as basic assumptions. The operations of a computer are much too rapid to observe or measure. Much of what goes on within a computer must be inferred and reconstructed from what we know about programs and electronics. Nonetheless, no one doubts the reality of what goes on within a computer nor the reliability of the results it can produce. And, not surprisingly, cognitive psychologists are now themselves beginning to talk about the "cognitive unconscious" although they still lack the developmental perspective.

One has to believe that writers like Hirsch (1987) and Bloom (1987) are fighting a rear-guard action for the old educational establishment. Hirsch, in particular, wants to deny the developmental perspective and assert that even young children can, and indeed should, be taught the most difficult subjects if they are to become "culturally literate." And Bloom also believes that if college students will only read the right books, all will be well with the world. Despite their humanistic coloration, both writers really reflect the behavioral version of learning and knowledge, that it is what you put into the student rather than what the student brings to the task of learning that is critical for education and true literacy. For both writers, it is the curriculum rather than the learner that is at the heart of their critique and why they remain wedded to the established paradigm. Ostensibly criticizing the paradigm, they instead reinforce it.

The existing paradigm remains well entrenched and is to some extent self-perpetuating. Professors suffused with this paradigm pass it on to their students, who then become professors of students, and so on. And the economic involvement of publishers adds to the entrenched position. When we recognize that the paradigm also supports educational programs that do not make the highest demands upon teachers and administrators, the commitment to the existing paradigm is understandable.

So, although progress is being made, the battle is far from won. Despite the fact that the signs of wear and tear on the old paradigm continue to mount, and although support for the new paradigm gathers strength and momentum, the tide has yet to turn. For the new paradigm to really take hold, something dramatic must happen. A new discovery in the realm of psychology, computer science, or education that will win the revolution is probably not going to happen. Breakthroughs in the social sciences are much less common than in the physical ones.

The pressure to accept the new paradigm will come from another quarter, most probably the economic. Another, more severe, stock market crash might finally move us toward education programs that reflect what we know about how children grow and learn. Not out of choice to be sure, but out of necessity. In the meantime, we must continue making our case for the developmental complexity of human thought and learning and its inaccessibility to direct observation and measurement. We must continue to advocate educational practice that sees the teacher as a learner alongside the child, rather than as a simple conduit of information. And we have to point out the social, economic, and political benefits that will accrue from an educational program that makes children enthusiastic, lifelong learners.

References

Bloom, Alan. *The Closing of the American Mind.* New York: Simon and Schuster, 1987.

Bloom, Benjamin S. *An Introduction to Mastery Learning.* Edited by J.H. Block. New York: Holt, Reinhardt and Winston, 1974.

Freud, S. "The Interpretation of Dreams." In *The Basic Writings of Sigmund Freud.* New York: Modern Library, 1938.

Hirsch, E.D., Jr. *Cultural Literacy: What Every American Needs to Know.* Boston: Houghton Miflin, 1987.

Kihlstrom, John F. "The Cognitive Unconscious." *Science* 237 (1987): 1441-1452.

Kuhn, Thomas S. *The Structure of Scientific Revolutions.* Chicago: University of Chicago Press, 1970.

Piaget, Jean. *The Psychology of Intelligence.* London: Routledge and Kegan Paul, 1950.

Skinner, B.F. *Beyond Freedom and Dignity.* New York: Knopf, 1971.

4
Quality in Early Childhood Education

DAVID P. WEIKART

Part of any solution to the prevention of major social and personal problems in adults is to provide high-quality preschool child development programs to them when they are young. This idea for prevention first became popular among leading educators and social scientists in the 1960s and led to the establishment of National Head Start. It also led to a variety of experimental programs and, in the spirit of the times, to a limited number of scientific evaluations of the effectiveness of these programs. Despite some early findings (Westinghouse Learning Corporation 1969) and some recent research (McKey et al. 1985) that cast doubt on the overall efficacy of the National Head Start program, the results of carefully drawn studies of preschool child development programs suggest a possible pattern of cause and effect that stretches from early childhood into adulthood (Berrueta-Clement et al. 1984).

Upon entering school, economically disadvantaged children are likely to perform less successfully than their middle-class peers because they have not developed to the same extent the skills, habits, and attitudes expected in kindergarten and 1st grade. This lack of development often manifests in low scores on tests of intellectual and scholastic ability, which can result in unnecessary (that is, preventable) placement in special education, retention in grade, low scholastic achievement, and, eventually, dropping out of high school.

Poor children who attend good preschool child development

programs become better prepared for kindergarten and 1st grade. Thus, they begin with a more successful experience in school, which will affect their adult lives. Perhaps the best known of these early intervention programs is High/Scope Foundation's Ypsilanti Perry Preschool Project (Berrueta-Clement et al. 1984).

The Perry Preschool Project

The Perry Preschool Project is an ongoing study that began in 1962. One-hundred twenty three black youths from families of low socioeconomic status, who were at risk of failing in school, comprise the study sample. The purpose of the study is to explore the long-term effects on these young people of either participation or non-participation in a high quality early childhood education program. Drawn from a single school attendance area, at ages 3 and 4 these youngsters were randomly divided into an experimental group that attended a high-quality preschool program and a control group that did not attend a preschool program. Information about these youngsters on hundreds of variables—including family demographics, child abilities, scholastic accomplishments, involvement in delinquent and criminal behavior, use of welfare assistance, and employment—has been collected and examined annually from ages 3 to 11; again at ages 14, 15, and 19; and then at age 28.

Curriculum

The Perry Preschool Project used the High/Scope Curriculum (Hohmann et al. 1979), an example of a high-quality early education program. Organized around Piagetian ideas, the fundamental premise of the curriculum is that children are active learners who construct their own knowledge from activities they plan and carry out themselves.

Active Learning by the Child

The High/Scope curriculum shares its emphasis on the child as active learner with historic early childhood methods like those of Froebel and Montessori. The main difference lies in its cognitive-developmental theoretical orientation, which places primary emphasis on problem solving, independent thinking, social development, and relationships. In the High/Scope model, teachers continually gauge the child's developmental status and present intellectual challenges intended to stretch the child's awareness and understanding.

The central principle of the High/Scope curriculum is that teachers must be fully committed to providing settings in which children actively learn through construction of their own knowledge. The child's knowledge comes from personal interaction with the surrounding world, from direct experience with real objects, from talking about experiences and ideas, and from the application of logical thinking to these events. The teacher's role is to support these experiences and help the child think about them logically.

Role of the Teacher

Through daily evaluation and planning, teachers study their experience with children and classroom activities and strive to achieve new insights into each child's unique tapestry of skills and interests. Additionally, teachers observe each other's performance and interact in mutually supportive ways.

An important aspect of the curriculum is the teacher's role in guiding the child's learning. While broad developmental milestones are used to monitor the youngster's progress, the teacher does not have a defined subject matter to teach. Instead, adults listen closely to what children plan and then actively work with them to extend the planned activities to challenging levels.

Adult questioning style is important. Adults ask for information from the youngster that helps the adult to understand and participate. "Test" questions about color, number, or size are rarely used. Instead, the adult emphasizes questions such as "What has happened?"; "How can things be made?"; "Can you show me?"; "Can you help another child?" The questioning style also permits free conversation between adult and child while modeling language for child-child interaction. This approach permits the teacher and the child to interact as thinkers and doers rather than in the traditional school roles of active teacher and passive pupil.

A Daily Routine to Support Active Learning

To create a setting in which children can learn actively, the daily classroom routine is consistent and varies only when the child has fair warning that things will be different the next day. This routine gives the child the control necessary to develop a sense of responsibility and to enjoy the opportunity to be independent. The daily routine in the High/Scope Curriculum is primarily a *plan-do-review* sequence, designed to give children opportunities to make choices about their activities while keeping the teacher intimately involved in the whole process.

Planning time. Planning time gives children a structured, consistent chance to express their ideas to adults and to see themselves as individuals who can act on decisions. They experience the power of independence and the joy of working with an attentive adult and peers.

As the teacher discusses plans with them, the children form mental pictures of their ideas and determine how to proceed. For adults, developing a plan with a child helps them not only to encourage and respond to the child, but to understand and gauge the child's level of development and thinking style. Both children and adults benefit: children feel reinforced and ready to start their plans; adults identify possible difficulties and where help may be needed.

Work time. The "do" part of the cycle is work time, the period after planning. It is generally the longest single period in the daily routine and is busy and active for children and adults alike.

Adults new to the curriculum sometimes find work time confusing because they are not sure of their role. Adults do not lead work-time activities—children execute their own plans of work—but neither do adults just sit back and passively watch. The adults' role during work time is to observe children to see how they gather information, interact with peers, and solve problems—and then to enter the children's activities to encourage, extend, and set up problem-solving situations.

Clean-up time. Clean-up time is wedged into the plan-do-review cycle in the obvious place—after the doing. During this time, children return materials and equipment to their places and store their incomplete projects. This restores order to the classroom and enables children to learn and use many basic cognitive skills.

Of special importance is how the classroom is organized to facilitate the child's use of materials. All materials in the classroom available for children are within reach on open shelves. Clear labeling is essential, usually with a direct representation of the objects stored on the shelf, to help children return work materials to their appropriate places.

Recall time. Recall time is the final phase of the plan-do-review sequence. The children represent their work-time experience in a variety of developmentally appropriate ways. They might recall the names of the children they involved in their plan, draw a picture of the building they made, or recount the problems they encountered. Recall strategies include drawing pictures, making models, and verbally recalling events. Recall time brings closure to planning and work-time activities. At this time, the teacher supports the linkage of the actual work to the original plan.

Small-group time. The format of small-group time is familiar to all preschool teachers: The teacher presents an activity in which children participate for a set period of time. These activities are drawn from the cultural background of the children, from group field trips, from the seasons of the year, and from age-appropriate group activities such as cooking and art projects. Although teachers structure the activity, children are encouraged to contribute ideas and solve problems in their own ways. They often work independently or in self-organized groups. Activities follow no prescribed sequence but reflect the children's needs, abilities, interests, and cognitive goals. Once each child has had the opportunity for individual choice and problem solving, the teacher extends the child's ideas and actions by asking open-ended questions and setting up additional problem-solving situations. Peer-to-peer discussion is encouraged.

Large-group circle time. At circle time, the whole group meets with an adult for 10 to 15 minutes to play games, sing, do finger plays and basic movement exercises, play musical instruments, or reenact a special event. Circle time allows each child to participate in a large group, share and demonstrate ideas, and share and imitate the ideas of others.

Results

When these 123 students were studied at age 19, differences were found between those who attended preschool and those who did not.

In education:

Fewer preschool graduates were classified as mentally retarded (15% vs. 35%)

More completed high school (67% vs. 49%)

More attended college or job training programs (38% vs. 21%)

In the world of work:

More preschool graduates held jobs (50% vs. 32%)

More supported themselves by their own (or spouse's) earnings (45% vs. 25%)

More were satisfied with work (42% vs. 26%)

In the community:
Fewer were arrested for criminal acts (31% vs. 51%)
More experienced a lower birth rate (64 vs. 117 per 100 women)
Fewer were on public assistance (18% vs. 32%)

Economic Outcomes

A cost-benefit analysis of 15 years of follow-up data from the Perry Preschool program showed a very positive value to taxpayers (Barnett 1984, Berrueta-Clement et al. 1984). The major cost of the program is the initial investment of about $5,000 per participant per program year (in constant 1981 dollars, discounted at 3 percent annually). It is important to note that this figure includes such items of school operation as building depreciation, clothing, and volunteers. Major benefits for the taxpayers were reduced costs of about $5,000 per participant for special education programs, $3,000 for crime, and $16,000 for welfare assistance. Additional postsecondary education for college and additional job training costs by participants added about $1,000 to costs. Participants were expected to pay $5,000 more in taxes because of increased lifetime earnings (predicted from their improved educational attainment).

Thus, total benefits to taxpayers amount to about $28,000 per participant, which is nearly six times the initial cost of the one-year program, or three times the cost of the two-year program. The return is large enough that even a two-year program that was only half as effective as the program studied would still yield a positive return on investment. The savings from reduced costs for special education alone are enough to return to taxpayers an amount equivalent to the cost of a one-year program.

Quality in Early Childhood Education

This success is not an endorsement of all early childhood programs. There is no intrinsic value in having a young child leave home for a few hours a day to join another adult and a group of children. Program quality must be carefully defined and maintained or a preschool classroom or child care center is just another place for a child to be. The positive effects of preschool programs have only been found for *high-quality child development programs.*

Having a high-quality program is not a matter of staff teaching degrees or financial or material resources; rather, it is the continued focus on the use of staff skills within a curriculum. It is the process of curriculum implementation that produces the results.

The High/Scope Preschool Curriculum Study addressed the issue of quality programming (Schweinhart et al. 1986) and provided some answers to the question, "Is one curriculum approach more effective than another?"

The High/Scope Preschool Curriculum Study

The ongoing High/Scope Preschool Curriculum Study began in the public schools of Ypsilanti, Michigan, in 1967. It served children 3 and 4 years old who lived in families of low socioeconomic status and who, according to test scores, were at risk of failing in school. To ensure the comparability of the groups, the children were randomly assigned to one of three curriculum models. The models all operated under similar administrative conditions and adhered to high standards of quality: a clearly articulated curriculum, ongoing training and supervision of staff, highly trained teachers, low teacher-pupil ratios, extensive parent involvement, and adequate resources. Yet they represented three major, theoretically distinct approaches to preschool programs. They differed in the degree of initiative expected of the child and the teacher—whether the child's and the teacher's primary roles were to initiate or to respond.

The *programmed-learning approach*—the teacher initiates activities to which the child responds. This was represented by the direct-instruction preschool program developed by Bereiter and Englemann (1966) and later published as DISTAR. Classroom activities are clearly defined academic skills with forceful positive child management procedures.

The *open-framework approach*—teacher and child both plan and initiate activities and actively work together. This was represented by the High/Scope Curriculum (Hohmann et al. 1979). Developed in the Perry Preschool Project, classroom activities revolve around key experiences intended to promote intellectual and social development. The underlying psychological theory is cognitive-developmental, as exemplified in the work of Piaget.

The *child-centered approach*—the child initiates and the teacher responds. This was represented by a nursery school program that incorporated the elements of traditional nursery school practice. Classroom activities are the teacher's responses to the child's expressed needs and interests. The teacher encourages children to actively engage in free play.

Of the 68 youngsters in the program, 54 were interviewed at

age 15—a retention rate of 79 percent. Previous data collections from ages 3 to 10, which took place either in the preschool programs or in the school, had retention rates of 90 percent or better. Comparisons on the designated characteristics of the remaining sample at age 15 to the original sample characteristics indicate that the age-15 sample was virtually equivalent to the original sample in every respect.

On self-report ratings of social behaviors, there were significant differences between the DISTAR group and the High/Scope and nursery school groups. On the delinquency scale, the DISTAR group reported a highly significant rate of juvenile delinquency when compared to the other two groups. The average member of the DISTAR group at age 15 engaged in 13 self-reported delinquent acts (girls, 14; boys, 12); the average nursery school group member engaged in 7 (girls, 7; boys, 7); and the average High/Scope member engaged in 5 (girls, 4; boys, 8). On all but 1 item of the 18-item delinquency scale, the DISTAR group reported the highest frequency, or was tied for the highest frequency, of the three groups.

Curriculum groups at age 15 did not yet manifest statistically significant differences in official contact with the police. Regardless of curriculum group, half the members of the sample reported having been picked up or arrested by police by age 15; the average sample member reported contact with the police 0.5 times, while average self-reported delinquency acts for the total sample was 8. In the Perry Project, police arrests "caught up" with self-reported delinquency by age 19. That is, the arrest rates closely paralled the rates of self-report acts of delinquency.

Family relations, activities, school behavior and attitudes, and mental health were also studied at age 15. The differences found in these areas suggest greater problems experienced by the DISTAR group than the other two. For example, 1 out of 3 members of the DISTAR group said their families felt they were doing poorly, a response made by only 1 out of 36 members of the other 2 curriculum groups combined.

To summarize the group differences among the children at age 15, then, more of the DISTAR group members reported they were not socially well adjusted, compared to both the High/Scope and the nursery school groups. Clearly, these data from this longitudinal, small-sample study suggest that there are social consequences to curriculum choice.

Implications

It is poor policy to finance preschool programs at per-child levels insufficient to provide high-quality programs. With limited funds, it is probably better to provide high-quality programs to only a few children than to provide inferior programs to a larger number of children. This has been the constant dilemma of the national Head Start project, which now serves only one in five eligible children. When quality is sacrificed to serve more children, the value of the program for all children may be seriously undermined.

If the purpose of preschool programs is to promote children's intellectual, social, and physical development, they must be conducted to meet high standards of quality by competent child development professionals who establish a nondirective environment that supports active learning by children. They should have the following characteristics of curriculum, staffing, and child and family services.

• A nondirective curriculum model, derived from principles of child development, that has been evaluated and found to have positive intellectual and social outcomes.

• Two adults for each classroom group and a classroom enrollment of no more than 20 children.

• Teaching staff members who are early childhood specialists with bachelors' degrees in early childhood development, child development associate credentials (usually a two-year degree) or equivalent, or staff members closely supervised by an experienced curriculum specialist.

• Support systems to maintain the curriculum model, including curriculum leadership by administration, curriculum-specific inservice training, supervision and evaluation procedures, and teaching staff assignments that permit daily team planning and evaluation of program activities.

• Collaboration between teaching staff and parents as partners in the education and development of children, including frequent communication and substantive conferences.

• Sensitivity and responsiveness to the child's health and nutrition needs and family needs for child care or other services.

With the enthusiasm of the newly converted, state and city governments have rushed to use the power of early education to reduce social problems. (See the booklet *Preventing Unemployment: A Case for Early Childhood Education* from the mayor's office in Minneapolis for the extent of such thinking). The business community has also become committed. (See the two publications of the Committee for Economic Development *Investing in Our Children* 1985 and *Children in Need* 1987.) High-quality early childhood programs have demonstrated their positive effect on students' lives, but such programs alone will not solve social problems. High-quality early childhood education—with an emphasis on quality—is the beginning to preventing major social and personal problems later in a student's life.

References

Barnett, W.S. *A Benefit-Cost Analysis of the Perry Preschool Program and Its Long-Term Effects.* Ypsilanti, Mich.: High/Scope Press, 1984.

Bereiter, C., and S. Englemann. *Teaching the Disadvantaged Child in the Preschool.* Englewood Cliffs, N.J.: Prentice-Hall, 1966.

Berrueta-Clement, J.R., L.J. Schweinhart, W.S. Barnett, A.S. Epstein, and D.P. Weikart. *Changed Lives: The Effects of the Perry Preschool Program on Youths Through Age 19.* (Monographs of the High/Scope Educational Research Foundation, 8). Ypsilanti, Mich.: High/Scope Press, 1984.

Committee for Economic Development. *Investing In Our Children.* New York: Author, 1985.

Committee for Economic Development. *Children in Need: Investment Strategies for the Educationally Disadvantaged.* New York: Author, 1987.

Hohmann, M., B. Banet, and D.P. Weikart. *Young Children in Action: A Manual for Preschool Educators.* Ypsilanti, Mich.: High/Scope Press, 1979.

McKey, R.H., L. Condelli, H. Ganson, B. Barrett, C. McConkey, and M. Plantz. *The Impact of Head Start on Children, Families and Communities* (Final Report on the Head Start Evaluation, Synthesis and Utilization Project). Washington, D.C.: CSR, 1985.

Minneapolis Community Business Employment Alliance. *Preventing Unemployment: A Case for Early Childhood Education.* Report on future employability. Minneapolis: Author, 1985.

Schweinhart, L.J., D.P. Weikart, and M.B. Larner. "Consequences of Three Preschool Curriculum Models Through Age 15." *Early Childhood Research Quarterly*, 1, 15-45, National Association for the Education of Young Children, 1986.

Westinghouse Learning Corporation. *The Impact of Head Start: An Evaluation of the Effects of Head Start on Children's Cognitive and Affective Development* (Vols. I-II). Athens, Ohio: Ohio University, 1969.

5
Kindergarten for Economically Disadvantaged Children: The Direct Instruction Component

DOUGLAS CARNINE, LINDA CARNINE,
JOAN KARP, PAUL WEISBERG

F
ive-year-olds enter school full of enthusiasm to learn. By the age of 16, however, they often seem to be negative, if not resentful, toward education. This metamorphosis is particularly marked in low-income children. The greatest challenge facing early childhood educators is to preserve children's positive attitudes toward school.

Many early childhood professionals believe that the solution begins with experience in a child-development oriented kindergarten program where students explore, select, and develop at their own pace. We contend that a kindergarten program for economically disadvantaged children must include effective academic instruction as well as child development experiences. While developmental activities meet some of the immediate needs of economically disadvantaged children, effective academic instruction anticipates the children's needs for competence and confidence in later grades.

The cycle of failure begins early for disadvantaged students. Eighty-two percent of the 4th graders scoring in the bottom quartile on standardized tests will not graduate from high school. But schools do not have to be powerless in breaking the link between poverty and failure. The intervention described in this chapter begins with 5-year-olds, when most public schools accept children. This intervention, called "direct instruction," focuses on students' academic competence. Most 5-year-olds from a low-income background enter school with far fewer skills and concepts than their more advantaged peers. Delaying academic instruction for disadvantaged students because they are not "ready" only widens the gap. Narrowing this performance gap requires early, intensive intervention.

The Kindergarten Child

Typical preschool programs for 4-year-olds are child centered. Children in these programs are usually given wide latitude in choosing what to do and experience virtually complete acceptance of their actions. A picture of scribbles is acknowledged for the pretty colors, a jangle of toy cymbals for the making of music; working with others to cut out figures and paste them together is cooperative problem solving. The goals are primarily participation, cooperation, and expression. Children explore, participate, express themselves, and develop trust, seeing school as a safe place outside the home. The child is a success. An important transition from home to school has begun.

In contrast, 1st grade is typically content centered. Reading, language arts, and mathematics require instructional time, which dictates the schedule. Children's choices are curtailed. More important, participation and expression are no longer sufficient to gain approval. A much narrower range of responses is acceptable. Reading the sentence "I saw a cat" as "Once upon a time" won't do; nor will calling a six "nine." We find that in the 1st grade, success and confidence slowly erode for many disadvantaged children.

Thus, kindergarten becomes a critical and sometimes difficult transition period from preschool to 1st grade. Kindergarten sets the stage for the child's school career and influences many other aspects of the child's life. Educators vary in their beliefs about what should happen during this transition. Some would like 1st grade to be more child-centered like preschool; others advocate a more content-centered approach. The resolution may be less crucial for children from affluent families than for children from low-income backgrounds. Without a well-orchestrated transition from a child-centered to a content-centered environment, children from low-income backgrounds may not be successful in 1st grade.

While kindergarten children need familiar activities, they must also experience success with content-centered activities. Although the kindergarten day is often no more than 200 minutes, both types of activities can be scheduled. The difficult task is planning and implementing the content-centered activities so that the students from low-income backgrounds will develop academic competence and positive self-esteem.

A Typical Direct Instruction Kindergarten Program

Intervention begins with an assessment of students' skills and knowledge to ensure that instruction begins at the appropriate level. Careful assessment takes into account each child's needs and developmental maturity, and helps the teacher place children in flexible ability groups. These ability groups of 6 to 12 students allow the children to progress more closely to their optimal rates. Group composition changes as the children's learning rates change.

The group activities are composed of short segments that focus on specific skills or combinations of previously taught skills. Teachers explain, demonstrate, and ask questions for 15 to 20 minutes in each subject area. These short segments closely approximate the attention span of kindergartners, capturing their interest through fast-moving and varied tasks. The lessons, which include frequent teacher-pupil verbal interaction through many games and races, provide the children with a great deal of active participation in the lessons and high engagement rates of as many as 10 responses per minute, with 80 to 90 percent of the responses being correct. Each lesson contains opportunities for the children to respond both as a group and individually.

Direct instruction can take as little as one hour a day. The teacher and a paraprofessional teach two groups concurrently while a third group works independently at learning or activity stations. Children at the activity stations might choose from a variety of child-centered activities such as building with blocks, looking at books, playing in the kitchen or at the sand and water tables, and working on the computer. A fine-motor and manipulatives table might be equipped with puzzles, crayons, and clay. The remainder of the daily schedule includes typical whole-group activities such as music, art, gross motor activities, and snacktime.

Direct Instruction Curriculum Content

The academic content of a Direct Instruction kindergarten program falls into the two main areas of language arts and mathematics. In the language arts, at least half of the instructional time is devoted to oral language instruction and practice. Important instructional words and concepts such as *and, or, same,* and *different;* comparatives; superlatives; and inferences are systematically introduced and taught. General knowledge concepts of time, space, location, and classification; part-whole relationships; occupations; colors; shapes; and patterns are also taught. Concept application activities synthesize earlier learnings. For example, students are shown the boxes in Figure 5.1 while the teacher states that the package with a ribbon *and* polka dot wrapping paper has paints in it. For each package the teacher then asks:

Does this package have paints in it?

Why did you give that answer?

For the first package, the students would answer, "Maybe, because it doesn't have polka dot wrapping paper." For the second package, the students would answer, "Maybe, because it doesn't have a ribbon." For the third package, the students would say, "Yes, because it has a ribbon *and* polka dot wrapping paper." The students have demonstrated an understanding of multiple attributes, inferences, and patterns.

Reading instruction is the second area of language arts instruction. Although the reading curriculum begins with discrete reading subskills such as sound-symbol identification, orally segmenting words, visual directionality, rhyming, and word reading, it is gen-

Figure 5.1

erally holistic. Very early in the program, students learn that reading is a tool to acquire information. As soon as students have acquired a few sound-symbols and blending strategies, they are given meaningful words in context to read. Although the subskills of the decoding process are taught in each lesson, an increasing amount of the student's time is spent using these skills to determine the meaning of words in context. Initially, students read short sentences and short simple stories. The stories are written with vocabulary words that are meaningful to the child and controlled for regularity to provide an opportunity to practice the sounds. The number of irregular words in the stories is kept to a minimum to reduce confusion about sound-symbol relationships. Reading a wider range of stories, including ones that the children have written themselves, is scheduled for later in the year. The children are encouraged to take all stories home and read them to their families.

Probably the major difference between the direct instruction and traditional reading readiness program is the way students learn sound-symbol relationships. Direct instruction teaches sound-symbol correspondences directly. The students learn, for example, that the sound *mmmm* is represented by the symbol *m*. The letters are not introduced in alphabetical order but according to usefulness in creating words for the students. In addition, letters that are likely to be confused are separated. For example, "b" and "d" appear close together in the alphabet and cause most initial readers considerable confusion. They are separated by many lessons, which reduces confusion (Carnine 1981). Another difference is the way new letters are introduced and practiced. Each new letter is introduced on one day and then practiced for two or three consecutive days until it is mastered. Although this rate is slower than in any other major reading program, a faster rate would overwhelm many kindergarten students. Thus, faster-learning kindergarten students could be grouped to spend one day on each new sound. Each previously introduced sound is also reviewed in sound-symbol correspondence tasks and in word reading tasks in each lesson.

The distinctive characteristic of the math curriculum is that students practice a wide variety of skills every day. In a 20-minute lesson during the fall, students will count pennies, claps, and pictures of various objects, identify and write numerals, and rote count to larger numbers. In the spring, students learn specific steps to solve addition and subtraction equations, translate orally presented story problems into simple equations, and derive unknown facts from familiar facts. As is the case for the reading instructional program, the mathematics program has provisions for moving students through the material slowly enough so they master the content. This emphasis on mastery is not characteristic of basal mathematics programs.

Research on Direct Instruction

Before adopting a program, its expected effect on young children must be determined. As is often the case, educators would like to be able to turn to research findings for guidance, but this is difficult. The ideal requirements for research that guides education policy include having:
• a sufficiently large number of students, both experimental and control,
• data collection and analysis conducted by outsiders,
• a representative research setting,
• representative students,
• reasonably objective and reliable measures for major conclusions, and
• random assignment of students to an instructional program.
Research studies on school-based programs rarely meet all of these criteria. Educators are thus forced to weigh findings within the context of the adequacy of the research. For example, much of the recent attention to direct instruction in kindergarten stems from the research of David Weikart and his colleagues (e.g., Schweinhart et al. 1986). There are many reasons to be cautious in interpreting their data, even though they were able to randomly assign students to treatment. Nevertheless, only a dozen students completed both years of the direct instruction preschool program. The program was administered by Weikart and carried out by teachers he hired. The research setting was his lab school, located at the headquarters of his foundation. The major conclusions, based on self-reported data, were not collaborated by objective measures, and the data are only for 3- and 4-year-old children. His results do not address the education of 5-year-olds and therefore have no direct implications for kindergarten. In short, decisions about direct instruction for 5-year-olds should not be based on experiences of a dozen 3- and 4-year-olds in a laboratory school where self-reported data were gathered by developers of a rival program.

Findings from Independent Researchers

A quite different set of implications for organizing kindergarten emerges when we look at research findings involving thousands of 5-year-olds in public school kindergartens across the United States; where findings were based on more objective, reliable measures; and where data were collected by an outside, impartial agency. The National Follow Through Project included a 6-year study of 13 different approaches (including Weikart's High/Scope Program and direct instruction) to teaching economically disadvantaged students in kindergarten through 3rd grade. At the project's peak, 75,000 low-income children from 170 communities participated annually. A wide range of low-income communities was represented.

Two impartial, independent agencies conducted the evaluation of Follow Through. Stanford Research Institute collected the evaluation data and ABT Associates analyzed them (Stebbins 1976, Stebbins et al. 1977). Although a critique of those results (House et al. 1978) cited some research limitations, the major findings of the national evaluation stand in spite of its shortcomings (Bereiter and Kurland 1981-2), in part, because of the consistency of the findings over time and across different school districts. These findings indicate very different effects for the direct instruction and Weikart High/Scope programs for kindergarten students from low-income backgrounds.

Results: Normative Performance. A major objective of the Direct Instruction Follow Through Program was to bring the achievement levels of disadvantaged primary-grade students up to the national average. The ABT Reports provide median percentile scores by school(s) and by sponsor for four Metropolitan Achievement Test measures: total reading, total math, spelling, and language. The average of medians for the Direct Instruction projects (converted to percentiles) for students entering in kindergarten are presented in Figure 5.2. The direct instruction students who began in kindergarten are close to or at national norms on all measures. These positive findings were supported in interviews with parents, direct instruction students, and parents of students from other approaches (Haney 1977).

A second objective was to determine whether some approaches were more effective than others. Each school had the same amount of additional funding for each student to implement the chosen approach. As shown in Figure 5.3, the differences between the

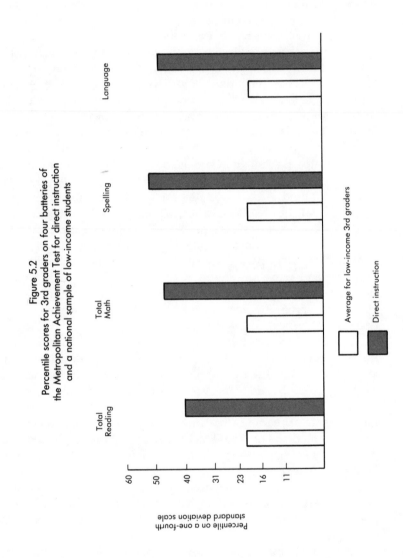

Figure 5.2
Percentile scores for 3rd graders on four batteries of
the Metropolitan Achievement Test for direct instruction
and a national sample of low-income students

□ Average for low-income 3rd graders

■ Direct instruction

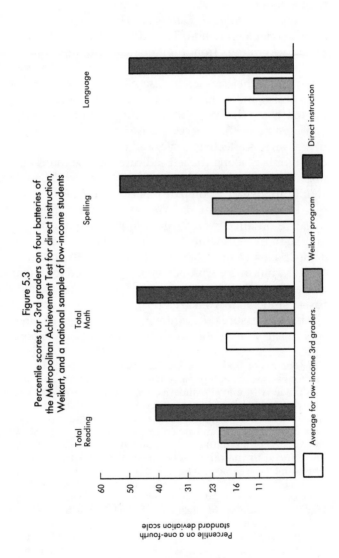

Figure 5.3
Percentile scores for 3rd graders on four batteries of
the Metropolitan Achievement Test for direct instruction,
Weikart, and a national sample of low-income students

Total Reading Total Math Spelling Language

Percentile on a one-fourth
standard deviation scale

60 50 40 31 23 16 11

☐ Average for low-income 3rd graders.   ▨ Weikart program   ■ Direct instruction direct instruction and the Weikart program were substantial in all four areas—one half standard deviation in reading, three-quarters of a standard deviation in spelling, and one and one-quarter standard deviation in math and language.

Results: Significant Outcomes. The results shown in Figure 5.3 have a serious limitation: They do not compare students of comparable backgrounds from the same communities. Stanford Research Institute anticipated that shortcoming and incorporated comparison groups into their research design. An overview of the percent of statistically and educationally significant differences between an approach and the comparison groups is found in Figure 5.4 (Becker and Carnine 1980).[1] The results are summarized across three groups of measures—affective, basic, and cognitive academic. Positive percent numbers along the left indicate more significant positive than negative comparisons; the negative percent numbers indicate more significant negative comparisons than positive.

The net effect of the Weikart program ranges from slightly negative on affective measures to strongly negative on basic skill and cognitive academic measures. Over a third of the academic comparisons were negative in terms of both statistical and educational significance. This means that compared to similar low-income students in traditional K-3 programs, in about one-third of the cases, students in Weikart's program scored significantly lower on academic measures. In contrast, the net effect of direct instruction was positive, with about one-third of the comparisons being posi-

---

[1]The major findings of the ABT Report are given in a series of tables, one for each sponsor. For each measure, a covariance adjusted comparison was made with a *local* comparison group and with a *pooled* national comparison group. When the mean for the Follow Through students exceeded the non-Follow Through mean by at least one-fourth of a standard devision on a given measure, and when the difference was statistically significant, this was considered an educationally significant outcome, and a plus (+) was placed in the table. When non-Follow Through exceeded Follow Through by the same criteria, it was considered to be a significant negative outcome, and a minus (−) was placed on the table. When the results fell between these limits, the difference was considered null and the table left blank. The number of pluses for Direct Instruction and for the Weikart program for each of the three types of measures was counted. (For the cognitive academic skills, the Raven's Progressive Matricies test, which is not an academic measure, was excluded.) Then the number of munuses was subtracted, and the result was divided by the number of comparisons. Both local and pooled comparisons were included. Decimals were converted to percents by multiplying by 100.

tive for academics and about one-fourth being positive for affective measures.

The affective findings from the ABT report are particularly noteworthy (Stebbins et al. 1977).

The performance of full time children in Direct Instruction sites on the affective measures is an unexpected result. The Direct Instruction model does not explicitly emphasize affective outcomes of instruction, but the sponsor has asserted that they will be the consequence of effective teaching. Critics of the model have predicted that the emphasis on tightly controlled instruction might discourage children from freely expressing themselves, and thus inhibit the development of self-esteem and other affective skills. In fact, this is not the case (p. 73).

While these results indicate a positive effect through 3rd grade for students who begin direct instruction in kindergarten, the opposite effect seems true for students in Weikart's program. One explanation is that Weikart's High/Scope Curriculum benefits only

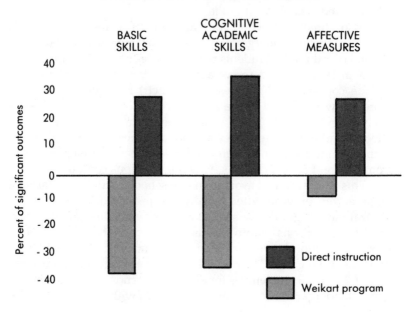

Figure 5.4
Percent of significant outcomes for 3rd graders on three types of measures across school districts for direct instruction and Weikart programs

3- and 4-year-olds, but not school-aged students. Another possible explanation comes from Weikart and his colleagues:

Previous research had found no outcome differences for programs lasting 1 year versus programs lasting 2 years . . . and extensive preliminary analysis of the data revealed no indication of program-duration effects in this study (Schweinhart et al. 1986, p. 22).

Shorter interventions with Weikart's High/Scope program may in fact be better than longer interventions.

Findings from Direct Instruction Researchers

Follow Through results for direct instruction and for Weikart's High/Scope program are for 3rd graders who entered school in kindergarten. The data provide information on comprehensive K-3 intervention, but little information about the relative contribution of the kindergarten year by itself. Partial answers to this question come from data gathered by direct instruction researchers. The first data are from comparisons of students who entered direct instruction during the kindergarten year with those who entered the program in 1st grade (Becker and Engelmann 1978). Third graders who entered school in kindergarten and spent four years in direct instruction scored significantly higher on achievement tests than students who entered school in 1st grade.

Also, direct instruction students with IQ scores below 71 who entered school in kindergarten gained an average of 17 IQ points by the end of 3rd grade. Students with IQ scores below 71 who entered school in 1st grade had an average gain of 9 IQ points. (These data include corrections for regression artifact.) For students with IQ scores between 71 and 90 the gains were between 16 and 9, respectively (Gersten et al. 1984). While these data suggest a powerful effect from kindergarten, they are not as conclusive as they might seem. The students who entered in kindergarten and 1st grade were from different school districts, which is a serious confound.

This confound was avoided in one school district that started a kindergarten program after initially starting the direct instruction program at 1st grade (Gersten et al. in press). This situation permitted comparisons within the same district of students who had direct instruction kindergarten with students who began direct instruction in 1st grade. The upper-left quarter of Figure 5.5 compares end-of-3rd-grade percentiles for direct instruction students who began in kindergarten (four-year intervention) with students who began in 1st grade (three-year intervention). The differences are substantial in all cases. The lower-left quarter of Figure 5.5 makes the same comparisons at the end of 9th grade. The advantages of beginning direct instruction in kindergarten are still evident at the end of 9th grade even though the students were in traditional programs for six years (grades 4 through 9).

The right side of Figure 5.5 lists the scores for the comparison students who were in school from kindergarten through 3rd grade or 1st grade through 3rd grade. The p values in parentheses indicate significant differences between direct instruction and comparison students. For example, direct instruction students who entered the program in kindergarten scored at the 56th percentile in mathematics at the end of 3rd grade. Comparison 3rd graders who entered school in kindergarten scored at the 26th percentile. This difference is significant at the .01 level. All the differences are significant for students who entered in kindergarten; only four of the six differences are significant for students who entered in 1st grade.

An interesting pattern found in the data for the comparison students (the right side of Figure 5.5) is that they also benefit from the extra year of kindergarten instruction. At both 3rd grade and 9th grade, kindergarten-beginning students scored higher than 1st-grade-beginning students, though the differences are much smaller by 9th grade. The differences between direct instruction students starting in 1st grade and students starting in kindergarten—at 3rd and 9th grade—suggest an enduring effect from the extra year of intensive instruction provided by a direct instruction kindergarten.

Other Longitudinal Research

Follow-up studies of direct instruction and comparison students were carried out in four other districts. All of the significant differences favored the direct instruction students: higher academic scores, better attendance, more college acceptances, and fewer retentions (Gersten and Keating 1987).

Research on Direct Instruction Preschools

Other researchers have conducted evaluations of direct instruction preschool programs for 4- and 5-year-olds. One large longitudinal evaluation was conducted by the Seattle public schools. A report that included this study was coauthored by Weikart's High/

Figure 5.5
Percentile scores for direct instruction and comparison students entering 1st grade and entering kindergarten at 3rd grade and 9th grade

	Direct Instruction Students		Comparison Students	
	Kindergarten (N=56)	1st Grade (N=96)	Kindergarten (N=45)	1st Grade (N=45)
3rd				
Reading	43	28	37 (.01)	28 (NS)
Math	56	36	26 (.01)	16 (.01)
Language	68	56	52 (.01)	20 (.01)
9th	(N=54)	(N=59)	(N=121)	(N=13)
Reading	40	23	26 (.01)	18 (.05)
Math	30	19	20 (.01)	18 (NS)
Language	59	42	39 (.01)	32 (.05)

(   ) indicate significant difference between Direct Instruction and comparison students

Scope Foundation. The 2,883 economically disadvantaged children who participated in Seattle's direct instruction preschool program

achieved better educational placements than a comparable control group. . . . Only 11 percent of these youngsters left high school before graduation, which is a dropout rate two-thirds the size of the control group's 17 percent dropout rate . . . had more than twice the percentage of students in gifted education and a rate of placement at or above the age-appropriate grade that was 10 percentage points higher than that of the control group (Schweinhart and Mazur 1987, pp. 18-19).

The findings on placement in gifted programs are particularly noteworthy. The percent for direct instruction students was about the same as for the district as a whole, 8 percent versus 9 percent. Yet 95 percent of the direct instruction students held minority status, while less than 50 percent of the students in the district as a whole held such status.

Another study was conducted by Weisberg at the University of Alabama (1987). Over nine years, 108 children—virtually all from low-income backgrounds, with 34 percent from families receiving public assistance and 14 percent living in foster homes—received one or two years of preschool instruction. The first finding was that students who received two years of direct instruction as 4-year-olds and 5-year-olds scored significantly higher on standardized reading achievement tests than students who had only one year of direct instruction. The extra year of instruction allowed the children to complete most of the second level of the direct instruction reading program. (During the second year of instruction, reading periods lasted 40 rather than 20 minutes.) The additional lessons seem largely responsible for the higher achievement of the students who had two years of instruction. In fact, the correlation between number of lessons completed and reading achievement was .92 ($p<.0001$), an extremely strong correlation.

The second finding stemmed from a comparison of students in direct instruction, cognitive development, Head Start, and no preschool programs. Students were given the standardized achievement test for the end of 1st grade at the beginning of 1st grade. As shown in Figure 5.6, the direct instruction students scored at or above the expected grade level for the *end* of 1st grade. Moreover, the direct instruction students scored significantly higher than students in all of the other groups. The direct instruction students' scores continued to be significantly higher than those of comparison students at the end of 1st grade and at the end of 2nd grade.

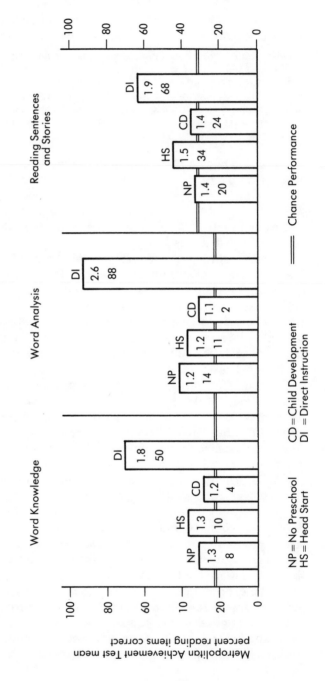

Figure 5.6

Percent correct reading subtest performance on the MAT for 1st grade starting age students. Top value in bar graph is grade equivalent score; bottom value is the percentile score on the test, not the percent correct.

NP = No Preschool   CD = Child Development   ═══ Chance Performance
HS = Head Start   DI = Direct Instruction

Research Summary

Taken as a whole, Weisberg's results in Alabama, the Seattle findings, and the Direct Instruction Follow Through results from over a dozen districts meet most of the criteria for research upon which to base policy decisions. They included large numbers of students, impartial data collection and analysis, representative settings and students, and reasonable measures. The results reflect the diverse benefits of well-implemented direct instruction programs: achievement gains, IQ gains, increased placement in gifted programs, reduced retention, reduced absenteeism, reduced dropout rates, and increased acceptance to college. The benefits are probably one-fifth of what is possible if students were to receive effective instruction after 2nd or 3rd grade. The possibilities would be enormous if students could receive careful, responsible instruction through 12th grade. In that case, direct instruction wouldn't even need to start in kindergarten. Unfortunately, implementing direct instruction is not easy, even in the primary grades.

The Components of Direct Instruction

That children from low-income backgrounds benefit from beginning direct instruction in kindergarten is evident across a variety of measures, both at the end of 3rd grade and in high school. The success of the students results primarily from the way content-centered activities are organized, including curriculum materials design, teaching techniques, time utilization, assessment of student performance, and staff development procedures.

Curriculum Design

Direct instruction curriculum materials (e.g., Mastery Reading, Mastery Spelling, DISTAR Language, DISTAR Arithmetic) are designed to engage the teacher and students in frequent verbal exchanges. The teacher gives a brief explanation, possibly models a skill, and then asks a series of quick questions to make sure the students understand the explanation. The teacher moves immediately to guided practice, again with frequent questions that prompt the steps that constitute the skill or strategy. Finally, students work independently. This process of modeling, guided practice, and independent practice works with various subject area content.

A much more challenging aspect of instructional design is specifying the explanations and questions. As Lee Shulman recently noted in his "Conversations from Wingspread" on PBS:

It is clear that the "nuts and bolts" approach is not enough: managing a classroom, handling discipline, using the bulletin board, working with the principal. All those things are important, but at least as important is the ability to take the content they're teaching and find the examples, the analogies, the demonstrations, the metaphors and the comparisons that will bring alive what is otherwise dead material. That is something you cannot do without having a very deep and rich understanding of teaching methods.

As paradoxical as it may sound, a deep and rich understanding of how to teach a subject requires an awareness of what students typically *mis*understand in the subject. For example, in beginning arithmetic, students will often write 8 as the answer to this missing addend problem: 3 + [ ] = 5. This error is common because in all previous problems, such as 3 + 5 = [ ] and 4 + 1 = [ ], students add two numbers and write the answer in the box. The cause of the error is a misunderstanding of the concept of equality; students do not understand that the equal sign sets off two sides that must have the same value. The sides must "balance."

The curriculum designer should plan around this potential misunderstanding. For example, in learning simple addition, such as 3 + 5 = [ ], students are required to put a ring around the side that tells how many: 3 + 5. They then use "counters" in following these steps.

• Make 3 lines for 3 and make 5 lines to show plus 5.
• Count all 8 lines.
• Indicate that they counted 8 on the side with 3 + 5, so they must count 8 on the side with the box (this is the equality rule).
• Write an 8 in the box.

These component skills are taught before students ae expected to chain them together to solve addition problems. Automaticity on component skills facilitates integration of the components into a more complex skill (Kameenui and Carnine 1986).

Once students become facile at simple addition problems, they are introduced to missing addend problems: 3 + [ ] = 5. The skill of circling the side that tells "how many" is now crucial. Students who circle 3 + [ ] are reminded that the box doesn't tell how many, so 3 + [ ] can't be the side that tells how many.

After students circle the side with 5 in 3 + [ ] = 5, they are asked to apply the equality rule: "I count five on this side, so I must count five on the side with three plus box." The teacher points out that there are already three on that side, so the students must count from three until they reach five. Each time they count, they make a mark under the box. Two marks under the box indicate that two have been added, so the students write a two in the box.

Student mastery of missing addend addition will grow out of the curriculum designer's anticipation of misunderstandings. This anticipation leads to preventive measures, which are built into the teaching of simple addition. Moreover, simple addition and missing addend addition employ the same component skills, further easing the transition to missing addend problems. In fact, the instructional design analysis also encompasses simple subtraction and missing subtrahend subtraction problems as shown in Figure 5.7.

Figure 5.7

Simple Subtraction

$7 - 3 = [\ \ ]$	Student circles side that tells how many.
$7 - 3 = [\ \ ]$	Student makes mark for the first number.
$7 - 3 = [\ \ ]$	Student minuses marks that must be removed.
$7 - 3 = [\ \ ]$	Student counts four remaining marks on side with $7 - 3$ and makes same number of marks on side with box.
$7 - 3 = [\ \ ]$	Student writes 4 in box.

Missing Subtrahend Subtraction

$7 - [\ \ ] = 4$	Student circles side that tells how many.
$7 - [\ \ ] = 4$	Student makes seven marks for first numeral.
$7 - [\ \ ] = 4$	Student circles four marks that must be counted on the side with $7 - [\ \ ]$.
$7 - [\ \ ] = 4$	Student minuses marks that must be removed.
$7 - [\ 3\ ] = 4$	Student counts how many marks were minused and writes the number in the box.

Note that the component skills are the same for addition, missing addend, missing subtrahend, and subtraction. This represents a tremendous efficiency that is particularly important for lower-performing students. They are more likely to succeed when they can learn certain skills and apply them in many different ways.

Efficiency and understanding are two overriding goals in instructional design, but they are often slighted in conventional basals. One mathematics basal introduced missing addend problems in this way.

The teacher was instructed to write these problems on the board.

$$9 + [\ \ ] = 10$$
$$9 + [\ \ ] = 11$$
$$9 + [\ \ ] = 12$$

The teacher then asked one student what number went in the box of the first problem. The teacher was then told to explain the second problem in the same way.

Teaching Techniques

The direct instruction teacher's guides specify the exact wording of explanations and questions that work well with a wide range of students. This allows teachers to focus their energy on presenting the material and helping students who have difficulties.

There are numerous empirically derived techniques for presenting direct instruction lessons to groups of students. For example, when students make a mistake in carrying out a multistep procedure, such as the one described for missing addend problems, the teacher reminds the students of the appropriate steps rather than just giving the correct answer. If students make this mistake— $4 + [10] = 6$—the teacher would remind them of the steps they've learned. First circle the side that tells how many. How many do you count on that side? So how many must you count on the side with four plus box? You've got 4. Count until you have 6. Make a mark for each number you count. Now write the answer that goes in the box.

When the teacher reminds students of the steps in the process, students receive helpful feedback about the process just when they need it, right after their mistake.

Time Utilization

A major problem facing kindergarten teachers is insufficient time to give children the individual attention they need. Having children sit at their desks for an hour or more and complete worksheets does not provide effective individualization. Young children need to interact with people, not sheets of paper, and teachers need to maximize the amount of time they spend with each child.

Direct instruction responds to this dilemma with a compromise: academic instruction is done in small groups in all subject areas, by both paraprofessionals and teachers. Paraprofessionals do not just run off dittos, prepare activities, and monitor seatwork; they *teach* one group of students while the teacher teaches a second. When paraprofessionals are not available, other options include recruiting volunteers to teach or making the instructional groups larger.

The other requirements of effective time utilization are familiar: schedule enough time for academic instruction, minimize interruptions, employ motivation techniques to keep students on-task, and cut wasted time in transition.

Assessment

Two forms of assessment are important in planning and implementing direct instruction in kindergarten. The first involves identifying children who particularly need intensive academic instruction; the second requires ongoing monitoring to identify students who are not learning successfully or at an acceptable rate.

Identifying eligible students. The process of identifying potentially at-risk 5-year-olds is about as reliable as identifying gifted 5-year-olds. It can be done only with a large margin of error. Some children from low-income backgrounds may learn academic skills rapidly even though they score poorly on readiness tests. Nevertheless, there are indicators that are reasonable predictors of later success in school.

A number of specific norm-referenced instruments for identifying at-risk students entering kindergarten are available. Measures such as Preschool Screening Survey (Hainsworth and Hainsworth 1980), Cooperative Preschool Inventory (Caldwell 1971), and the Boehm Test of Basic Concepts (Boehm 1971) provide valuable information for determining which kindergarten children might need a more systematic instructional program.

Some of the best predictors of kindergarten success are those that most closely match the activities children usually do in school (Keogh and Becker 1973). Informal assessments such as alphabet and numeral identification, knowledge of rote counting and object counting, fine motor tasks testing the ability to hold a pencil and copy marks can be used by the kindergarten teacher. For example, the average kindergarten child knows 13 letters of the alphabet when entering school (Anderson et al. 1985); therefore, students who can identify six or fewer letters may need extensive work. Especially worthy of consideration are students who have difficulty matching letters. Most kindergarten children can also identify at least five or six numerals. Those who identify four or fewer numerals may also need extensive intervention. Certainly children who have difficulty holding a pencil and writing or identifying letters in their names merit thorough assessment.

A simple, discriminating oral language task that can be used to identify at-risk students is verbatim statement repetition. A child is asked to repeat a long statement such as, "I go to the store to buy bread, butter, and milk" exactly as the examiner said it. Students who are unable to repeat the statement in four trials may be particularly good candidates for direct instruction.

Monitoring Student Progress. Criterion-referenced tests to monitor student (and teacher) performance are built into (or are available for) each direct instruction program. Items on these measures are designed to correspond to specific instructional tasks so that remedial implications are clear. Student performance on specific classes of items can define areas where additional instruction is required. Teachers and administrators can also use the results of these measures to identify areas where instruction is weak.

In addition to criterion-referenced tests, student progress is measured by content coverage, which is typically measured in terms of lessons. A high-ability group can cover an average of 1.2 to 1.5 lessons per day, and the lowest group at least .7 lessons per day. When groups progress more slowly than expected, teachers evaluate how time is being used in the classroom and can then reschedule activities to increase instructional time and work on behavior management techniques to improve the use of time.

Transportability

Direct instruction can work in diverse situations; this transportability is extremely important. Consider Thomas Edison, who is well known for inventing the light bulb. What we forget is that the light bulb is useless without a lamp or an outlet to plug in the light. Possibly a much greater accomplishment was Edison's engineering of the delivery system of electricity: power lines, transformers, and the like. Similarly, direct instruction is of only academic interest if we are not cognizant of its staff development requirements (Carnine and Gersten 1984) and the stages through which it must pass—awareness, planning, implementation and institutionalization (Carnine 1988). Understanding the requirements for staff development and the change process allows educators to successfully install and maintain major innovations such as direct instruction.

Schools seeking to improve kindergarten need programs that

have been validated in real-world public schools, with tenured teachers, far from a program developer's tutelage. For this to be possible, the educational program must be explicitly described with reasonable requirements for implementation. With scripted lesson plans; an intensive, continuous staff development program (Carnine and Gersten 1984); highly skilled local consultants; and other features, direct instruction is sufficiently explicit.

Being explicit does not make direct instruction simple or easy to implement. The thoroughness of the instructional programs and teaching procedures give teachers precise information about how each student is learning on a moment by moment basis. Responding quickly and constructively is extremely demanding. Similarly when students are moved too quickly or too slowly through the instructional programs, serious problems can result.

However, adequate implementation is quite feasible when teachers participate in appropriate staff development activities. This has been confirmed by the Department of Education Joint Dissemination Review Panel, which validates educational programs as exemplary models and qualifies them for national dissemination. During the 1980-81 school year, all 12 of the active Direct Instruction Follow Through projects were submitted for validation. Eleven of the 12 districts had 8 to 10 years of data on successive groups of children. The schools sampled a full range of students: large cities (New York, San Diego, Washington, D.C.); middle-size cities (Flint, Michigan; Dayton, Ohio; E. St. Louis, Illinois); rural white communities (Flipping, Arkansas; Smithville, Tennessee); a rural black community (Williamsburg, South Carolina); a Mexican American community (Uvalde, Texas); a Spanish American community (E. Las Vegas, NM): and an American Indian community (Cherokee, North Carolina). All of the projects were certified as exemplary in reading and mathematics for the primary grades, thus providing replication over 8 to 10 years and in a dozen quite diverse communities.

Expectations

Direct Instruction can benefit students in a number of lasting ways. These accomplishments are quite difficult to achieve, however. The cycle of failure found in many low-income neighborhood schools must be broken in staff members before it can be broken in the students. Yet, staff members will not, and should not be expected to, change their expectations until they see their students succeed. It's a circular problem: higher expectations come from demonstrations that the expectations are reasonable; yet demonstrations that students can succeed require increased expectations. The resolution of this contradiction requires true educational leadership. The leader must create an environment that leads to success for both the staff members and the students—bringing to bear appropriately designed curricular materials, effective teaching techniques, all available time for instruction, a system for identifying eligible students and monitoring their progress, and intensive staff development. Often, teachers resist major changes such as those represented by direct instruction. However, most teachers accept the program once they see the results (Gersten et al. 1986).

The most impressive results involve personal experiences with students like Antonio. Antonio was the shyest student in his direct instruction kindergarten class. He would not talk in a group for the first month and only then would whisper his answers. The teacher called on him each day and accepted his responses and encouraged him when he did answer. In April, one of the teachers from a non-direct instruction classroom came down the hall and said to the direct instruction kindergarten teacher, "I understand that your children can read. I would like to hear them." Antonio overheard the conversation and spontaneously said in a loud voice, "You want to hear me read." He promptly and proudly read her a passage from his book.

Stories like this are too rare because school administrators and parents are too distracted or too cautious to create the necessary environment for change (Carnine 1988). The cliche "no guts, no glory" aptly describes the challenge and the failure of school administrators and parents in low-income schools. Phrased more mildly, if the problem were easy to solve, it would have been solved long ago. Remember though, we are the problem, not the children.

References

Anderson, R.C., E.H. Hiebert, J.A. Scott, and I.A.G. Wilkinson. *Becoming A Nation of Readers*. Washington, D.C.: National Institute of Education, 1985.

Becker, W.C., and D.W. Carnine. "Direct Instruction—An Effective Approach to Educational Intervention with Disadvantaged and Low Performers." In *Advances in Child Clinical Psychology: Vol. 3*, edited by B. Laney and A. Kazdin. New York: Plenum, 1980.

Becker, W.C., and S. Engelmann. "Analysis of Achievement Data on Six Cohorts of Low Income Children from 20 School Districts in the University of Oregon Direct Follow Through Model." Unpublished manuscript, Follow Through Project, Technical Report #78-1. Eugene: University of Oregon, 1978.

Bereiter, C., and M. Kurland. "A Constructive Look at Follow Through Results." *Interchange* 12 (1981-2): 1-22.

Boehm, A.E. *Boehm Test of Basic Concepts*. New York: Psychological Corporation, 1971.

Caldwell, B.M. *Cooperative Preschool Inventory*. Princeton, New Jersey, 1971.

Carnine, D.W. "Barriers to Improving Reading Instruction." In *Building Exemplary Reading Programs and Initiating Changes*, edited by S.J. Samuels and P.D. Pearson. Newark, Del.: International Reading Association, 1988.

Carnine, D.W. "Reducing Training Problems Associated with Visually and Auditorily Similar Correspondences." *Journal of Learning Disabilities* 14 (1981): 276-279.

Carnine, D.W., and R. Gersten. "The Logistics of Educational Change." In *Reading Education: Foundations for a Literate America*, edited by J. Osborn, P.T. Wilson, and R.C. Anderson. Boston: D.C. Heath, 1984.

Gersten, R., W.C. Becker, T.J. Heiry, and W.A.T. White. "Entry IQ and Yearly Academic Growth of Children in Direct Instruction Programs: A Longitudinal Study of Low SES Children." *Educational Evaluation and Policy Analysis* 6, 2 (1984): 109-121.

Gersten, R., D. Carnine, L. Zoref, and D. Cronin. "A Multifaceted Study of Change in Seven Inner City Schools." *Elementary School Journal* 86, 3 (1986): 319-331.

Gersten, R., C. Darch, and M. Gleason. "The Effectiveness of Academic Kindergartens for Low Income Students: Analysis and Discussion." *Elementary School Journal*. In press.

Gersten, R., and T. Keating. "Improving High School Performance of 'At Risk' Students: A Study of Long-term Benefits of Direct Instruction." *Educational Leadership* 44 (March 1987): 28-31.

Hainsworth, P.K., and M.L. Hainsworth. *Preschool Screening System*. Pawtucket, R.I.: ERISYS, 1980.

Haney, W. *Reanalysis of Follow Through Parent and Teacher Data*. Boston: Huron Institute, 1977.

House, E.R., G.V. Glass, L.D. McLean, and D.E. Walker. "No Simple Answer: Critique of the 'Follow Through' Evaluation." *Harvard Educational Review* 48 (1978): 128-160.

Kameenui, E., and D. Carnine. "Preteaching Versus Concurrent Teaching of the Component Skills of a Subtraction Algorithm to Skill-Deficient Second Graders: A Component Analysis of Direct Instruction." *The Exceptional Child* 33, 2 (1986): 103-115.

Keogh, B.K., and L.D. Becker. "Early Detection of Learning Problems: Questions, Cautions and Guidelines." *Exceptional Children* 40 (1973): 5-11.

Schweinhart, L.J., and E. Mazur. *Prekindergarten Programs in Urban Schools*. Ypsilanti, Mich.: High/Scope Foundation, 1987.

Schweinhart, L.J., D.P. Weikart, and M.B. Larner. "Consequences of Three Preschool Curriculum Models through Age 15." *Early Childhood Research Quarterly* 1, 1 (1986): 15-35.

Stebbins, L. (Ed.) *Education Experimentation: A Planned Variation Model (Vol. IIIA).* Cambridge, Mass.: ABT Associates, 1976.

Stebbins, L., R.G. St. Pierre, E.L. Proper, R.B. Anderson, and T.R. Cerva. *Education Experimentation: A Planned Variation Model (Vol. IVA-D).* Cambridge, Mass.: ABT Associates, 1977.

Weisberg, P. "Accelerating the Reading Achievements of Poverty-Level Preschoolers by Extensive Training in Synthetic Phonics." Tuscaloosa: University of Alabama, 1987.

6
Analysis of Issues Concerning Public School Involvement in Early Childhood Education

ASCD EARLY CHILDHOOD EDUCATION POLICY PANEL

I n analyzing the issues surrounding early childhood education, the ASCD policy panel had a two-fold goal: to promote
high-quality public school programs and to provide guidance
to school leaders in establishing and revising their programs.
The issues addressed here focus specifically on public school
programs for 4- and 5-year-old children because it is urgent to for-
mulate appropriate, carefully conceived, and forward-looking policy
for the youngest and most recent entrants into the public schools.

Historically, public education in the United States has been
provided in response to social trends and society's needs. Universal
public education was initially a response to the need to eliminate
child labor abuse and assimilate massive numbers of immigrants
into American society. Similarly, federal programs for young children in the 1930s, '40s, and '60s responded to problems of the
Depression, World War II, and poverty.

Day, in chapter 1 of this book, describes current social, demographic, and economic trends, as well as empirical research data

regarding the effectiveness of early childhood programs, that have today created a clear and compelling demand for the public schools to respond with "high-quality" programs. Our at-risk students need more than intervention; providing them with sound, effective programs not only increases their chances for success throughout life, it provides enduring benefits for society as well.

Fortunately, the public schools have the capacity to develop high-quality early childhood education. They already have many of the resources needed to operate sound programs for young children. They already have a knowledge base about young children, physical facilities, administrative systems, and professional staffing procedures, all of which are needed to develop an early childhood curriculum and to operate programs for 4- and 5-year-olds. The public schools also have the advantage of credibility in the community and well-established connections with parents, local government, and other community agencies.

Several recent reports related to the effectiveness of the public schools (e.g., *A Nation at Risk* and the Carnegie Report) fuel an assertion that since the public schools have ruined K-12 education, they cannot be trusted with programs for 4-year-olds. This assertion is negated by outcomes from public schools and reports of public opinion. At the outset, it must be recognized that American public schools are charged with the responsibility of educating all children, regardless of academic ability or inclination. Nathan (1986, p. 198-199) discusses a report from the National Governors' Association on educational issues: "Governors know that education has made progress. Over the last 30 years, the high school graduation rate in the United States has risen from about 50 percent to above 75 percent. Students' scores on tests of basic skills are also on the rise." In September 1986, the *Phi Delta Kappan* (pp. 46-47) reported on a Gallup poll about public attitudes toward public schools. When asked to grade their local schools, 41 percent of the respondents gave grades of A or B, while only 5 percent gave a failing grade. Sixty-five percent of those questioned about the schools their children attended responded favorably. The general public does not feel that schools have failed.

In this atmosphere, with existing capacities and adequate funding, today's educators can assume the responsibilities of developing and implementing high-quality early childhood education programs.

Providing High-Quality Programs

Providing a successful and worthwhile early childhood program is a major challenge. It requires careful examination of many controversial issues including teacher preparation and instructional strategy. It requires careful planning and decision making about funding, program goals, and populations to be served.

Scope of the Program

Currently in the United States, there is a trend toward mandatory kindergarten attendance—eight states as of 1987—and toward longer school days for kindergarten children—14 states with school days up to six hours (Robinson 1987). One issue facing policy makers is whether to more fully serve 5-year-olds before they begin or expand efforts to serve younger children. In chapter 1 of this book, Day notes that the majority of kindergarten programs operate for less than 3.5 hours per day, as do most programs for 4-year-olds. School-day length is a major factor that will determine the scope of programs for 4- and 5-year-olds in public schools. The question of whether programs should operate on a longer schedule, either a full school day (5-6 hours) or an extended day to meet parents' working hours, is often debated in terms of whether the mission of programs is to provide education, child care, or both.

Some schools have argued that a longer day would be too demanding and stressful for 4- and 5-year-old children (Brandt 1986). Yet many children spend a full day in child-care settings. A longer day has the advantage of reducing stress on children caused by having to move from one facility to another. With a full-day program there is no need to hurry through learning activities on a two- to three-hour schedule (Brandt 1986). In addition to these practical aspects, some research studies show that children can and do prosper in full day programs (Murray 1987, Puleo 1986).

Defined in the narrowest terms possible, education refers to academic skills instruction; child care involves custodial and protective services. However, such a distinction is inaccurate and inconsistent with the needs of young children and their families. Public schools already provide many services to K-12 students beyond the narrow definition of education (e.g., nutrition programs, medical screening, and counseling), and high-quality child care services include educational components (Caldwell 1986). The more useful consideration is to provide appropriate education and care for children, regardless of the setting.

Thus, the central question is what type of program is appropriate. When the artificial distinction between education and care is removed, public schools can provide children with an experience-based program that includes individual and group activities, structured and unstructured play, time for listening, sharing stories, resting, and the opportunity to be in a safe and stimulating environment for as long as their parents are at work.

Who Should Attend

An essential issue is whether or not public school programs for 4- and 5-year-olds should be limited to children who are at risk of academic failure—those who are economically disadvantaged or have special needs. Due to funding constraints, the majority of the public school programs now available are for at-risk children only, which has often created segregated situations. The child with special needs is usually served only with other such children, and the economically disadvantaged are often segregated by race or class.

While it is appropriate to serve at-risk children first, it is important to include other children as soon as possible. Most of the research has been conducted with at-risk populations, but a few studies have also demonstrated positive effects without regard to socioeconomic status (Durkin 1974-75, Hanson 1987). There are, in fact, educational advantages to mixed socioeconomic groupings since young children learn from one another (Coleman et al. 1966, Abelson et al. 1974, Johnson and Johnson 1985). Many early childhood professionals have called for programs for all children. "The best programs provide an integrated setting with children of various racial and socioeconomic backgrounds, rather than segregating at-risk children from others" (Grubb 1987).

Another issue is whether prekindergarten programs should be voluntary or mandatory. Even if mandatory prekindergarten programs were feasible, parents should still retain the right to decide whether their young children should attend.

Evaluation of Children

The validity of using tests with young children and of the tests themselves has been a long-standing issue. The best solution provides for individual testing of each child, acceptable administration and scoring practices, knowledge of child growth and development, and caution in interpreting results. In this process, no one test is adequate to diagnose the strengths and needs of a young child or to determine placement in a readiness for transition classroom or eligibility for school enrollment (Gadson 1980). Instead, test results, teacher observation, parent-provided information, and data from other professionals (e.g., medical history) should be combined to create a profile for determining how best to meet a child's needs.

Caution must be applied in interpreting the results of diagnosis, assessment, or evaluation. Parents or teachers may use their understanding of the profile to expect children to achieve at a level far beyond or below their capacity. Adults who expect too much or too little frustrate children and thwart their growth.

Comprehensive early identification should involve all the school specialists and the parents and provide any necessary inservice training to teachers. The early identification process should provide better information for staff regarding what children need, and this in turn should be shared with the parents. In so doing, the parents and the schools come together in a partnership for children.

Funding Sources

A critical, fundamental issue in establishing and expanding public school programs for 4-year-olds is who will pay. One answer is that everyone pays and that the real question is who pays, how much, when, and for what. It costs a significant amount of money to educate and nurture young children. Yet it costs much more to remediate later and even more to address the problems of crime, undereducation, abuse, dropouts, welfare, and other social ills. The Perry Preschool Program's cost-benefit analysis (Barnett 1985) points the way in describing why an early expenditure is highly beneficial later.

The Committee for Economic Development's 1987 report estimated that it would cost about $3 billion annually to provide high-quality prekindergarten programs for all of our nation's at-risk 4-year-olds. The major potential funding sources for programs for all children, especially those from low-income families, are federal, state, and local governments. Private enterprise and parent fees, rather than tax dollars, are potential funding sources for programs for children who are not at risk.

Currently, federal funding is provided largely through the Head Start program ($1.113 billion), through Social Services Block Grant funds ($2.7 billion) for child care, and through Public Law 99-457 for early intervention with handicapped infants and toddlers ($67 million); all are targeted exclusively for at-risk groups. The Act for

Better Child Care, if passed in the 1988 Congress, could add $2.5 billion in support for child care. However, these programs are far from meeting the need—over 80 percent of our nation's economically disadvantaged children do not receive Head Start services.

The major funding initiatives for new and expanded programs for 4-year-olds come from the states. Currently, 24 states fund prekindergarten programs, and another 4 either allocate money to supplement Head Start programs or to fund parent education programs (Marx and Seligson 1987). As with federal funding, however, state funding is far from meeting the need. The funding among states that operate prekindergarten programs varies considerably from a high of $64.5 million in Texas to a low of $83,000 in Ohio for pilot programs (Marx and Seligson 1987).

A survey by Schweinhart and Mazur (1987) of 28 of the 38 members of the Council of the Great City Schools reports that the 1985-86 enrollment in public school prekindergarten (69,964) was 23 percent of the enrollment in kindergarten (305,885). Funding sources that year were 36 percent federal, 35 percent state, and 29 percent local. Over half of these respondents indicated that prospects for new state or local funds appeared good or very good.

It is unrealistic to expect any one source to bear the costs of providing high-quality, comprehensive programs. Although fewer than one-third of the states require local level coordination among public schools, child care programs, and other services for prekindergarten children (Marx and Seligson 1987), collaboration in planning, funding, and using resources efficiently will be essential in reaching families who want and need high-quality early education and care for their children. Examples of collaboration include multidistrict cooperatives that can reduce overhead and start-up costs and public school/nonprofit organization agreements for transportation and other services. Local coordination, as well as the flexibility to utilize community providers, is imperative in stretching the available resources to reach the greatest possible number of children.

Other sources of funds are public and private employers who have a vested interest in supporting the development of high-quality programs for the children of their workers. Of the approximately 6 million corporations in the United States, about 3,000 provide some kind of child care assistance for employees (NAEYC undated), a 50 percent increase since 1984 (Chapman 1987). An example of the kind of collaboration that can and should occur is the consortium of corporations and government agencies that the BankAmerica Foundation has underwritten with a $1.1 million budget to make better child care available in five California counties (Chapman 1987). Such efforts can be particularly useful in expanding programs to include the children of corporate employees. Another example, spearheaded by Proctor & Gamble in Cincinnati, is the effort to expand high-quality prekindergarten programs in collaboration with the Cincinnati Public Schools. The Cincinnati Youth Collaborative (or Cincinnati United for Youth) was organized by a corporate executive who wanted to make a positive change for children, who are the future adults and workers of the city. A group of city officials, public school leaders, and corporate executives is focusing on areas such as developing prekindergarten education for at-risk youngsters, improving the school system's instructional programs, building bridges from schools to jobs and from schools to colleges, and developing dropout prevention programs (Pepper 1987).

Funding of programs for young children should be designed to complement and support families, not to replace family responsibilities. A sliding fee scale is one way to accomplish this goal. The fee may vary from zero dollars to the full cost per child, depending on a family's ability to pay. Edward Zigler (1987) has suggested the sliding fee scale as an option for implementing child care as part of the public school system.

Appropriateness of the Program

Determining appropriate program goals, content, structure, and instructional strategies is a critical, substantive, and divisive issue in the field. Early childhood education programs are typically characterized as "academic" or "developmental," depending on whether the stated focus is growth in academic skills or growth across a broad range of developmental areas, including the cognitive, physical, social, and emotional domains. Such labels are of little use, however, in determining program appropriateness. A high-quality early childhood program supports the growth of academic skills as an integrated part of the child's total development.

Academic Focus. In academically focused programs, the teacher clearly defines the content of the day's academic sessions. Children are provided with a sequenced series of activities that gradually build competence in reading, language concepts, and understanding of basic number concepts. Instruction is deliberate and systematic, and children practice using newly taught concepts. These concepts and skills are further reinforced during the unstructured portions of the program. The teacher in a half-day program ordinarily combines 90 minutes of academic instruction with 90 minutes of other activities.

Although teachers, not children, determine the objectives of each day's systematic lesson, in *good* academic early childhood programs children are actively involved. The majority of instruction is conducted in small groups, with a small amount of follow-up worksheet activities. Children constantly respond to teachers' questions and to each others' comments. They receive clear and immediate feedback on their responses and are provided with additional practice if necessary. Good academically focused programs also include time for play, socialization, and art.

Developmental Focus. Proponents of the developmental focus emphasize that their programs fit the way young children learn in general and accommodate the specific developmental needs, abilities, and interests of individual children. Knowledge about how young children learn is the key to operationalizing this standard. Seefeldt (1985) argues that the kindergarten classroom must involve a curriculum that has play and language activities that accommodate different rates of child growth and development. Young children begin to construct meaning from concrete experience with the materials, objects, and people in the world around them. They learn primarily through sensory experience and action—exploring, manipulating, creating, dismantling, and reconstructing things in their environment. Children grow cognitively and socially through collaborating with others, discussing their actions, restructuring and analyzing their actions to discover "why" and "how," and applying what they are learning in ways that are personally meaningful. Knowledge and concepts develop through reconstruction of actions, activities, and interactions. Whatever is taught or told to the young child is understood in direct proportion to the sum of that child's related experience (Cowles 1974).

The learning activities within developmental programs are highly experiential, involving active exploration of the classroom environment, guided discovery, concrete experiences, and structured and unstructured play. Academic skills are developed within this framework, and a variety of formats is used for the learning activities, including independent activity and teacher-led, small-group instruction. The role of the child in such a program is active/

initiating: choosing activities of interest and working with teacher guidance in planning, carrying out, and evaluating learning activities (Day and Drake 1983, 1986, Day 1988).

Research on the efficacy of academically and developmentally focused programs indicates that both types can produce significant gains in IQ score, academic achievement, and general school success (Schweinhart et al. 1986, Gersten and Keating 1987). The implication for policymakers is that no one approach or program type is best; children learn best through a variety of approaches that are chosen to meet their individual needs.

A wide range of effective prekindergarten and kindergarten programs (e.g., Weikart in chapter 4, Carnine in chapter 5, Katz in chapter 2, Day and Drake 1986, Gersten et al. in press) have in common the following components.

• Small-group, total-group, and individual activities.
• Both teacher-directed and child-initiated activities.
• Time allotted each day for skills groups based on children's abilities.
• Language development opportunities—including both speaking and listening comprehension.

These components are intentionally broad and avoid unresolved controversy over philosophical issues and the relative merits of specific program models. The list is intended to serve as a set of basic elements of effective programs. If a program does not require much work in the area of language development, or if it relies exclusively on individualized, one-on-one activities without any small group activities, there is a good chance the program is unbalanced and should be revised. The developmental and experiential program described by Day and Drake (1983, 1986) is a good example of the application of these common components. In it children spend one-third of each day on independent activities planned by the teacher, one-third in teacher-directed small-group instruction, and one-third in free choice activities.

Should Children be Taught to Read?

A common controversy in curriculum design revolves around the relative importance of language and social development as opposed to learning to read and write. The essential issue is how children learn and when they should be taught certain skills. Seefeldt (1985, p.14) articulates what all educators agree upon: "The ability to read requires a solid foundation of oral language." Oral language components, such as communication, expression, and reasoning, can be facilitated through conversation in small groups of three or four in the early childhood classroom (Katz chapter 2).

It is important, then, to provide opportunities for children to have much verbal interaction with one another and with adults on a one-to-one basis. Teachers can provide such opportunities as they elaborate and qualify their answers to children's questions; read aloud from a variety of materials; and make tapes, records, books, and pictures available. It is important, however, that the teacher provide opportunities for the children to talk about what they hear and see (Leeper et al. 1984, pp. 211-212).

Although most 5-year-olds *can* learn to read, the question that requires conscious decision making at the local level is whether they *should* learn to read. For 5-year-olds who are still working on fine motor skills (speaking, eye/hand coordination) or socialization (to the extent to which it is needed to enhance language), learning to read can be deferred until mastery of these preparatory skills is achieved. On the other hand, the longitudinal evaluation of Project Follow Through demonstrated that many low-income minority students can be taught to read in kindergarten, regardless of scores on readiness tests or other developmental measures (Gersten and Keating 1987). The decision to begin formal reading instruction and at what age to begin it must be based on an analysis of the needs and abilities of each child and ongoing evaluation of whether these needs are being met.

Advocates of teaching reading instruction in kindergarten argue that many 5-year-olds can be taught to read if the materials used are age-appropriate, if the teaching is highly interactive, and if the teaching is organized in such a way that all children experience success daily (Gersten et al. 1982, Meyer 1984). Four critical components appear essential to an effective reading program for 5-year-olds. First, the curriculum should be geared to the developmental level and attention span of 5-year-olds, involving a good deal of oral practice and a high rate of teacher-child interaction. Selected Follow Through kindergartens used lessons consisting of a series of brief three- to five-minute segments. Each skill was broken down into very small steps. Care was taken to ensure that this was not a "watered down" 1st grade reading program, but rather a program uniquely developed for 5-year-olds (Engelmann and Bruner 1978, Engelmann and Osborn 1976). Second, the program must be taught in such a way that all children experience success (Gersten et al.

1982). Third, the program must combine and integrate practice in specific reading skills with more holistic comprehension activities. Teachers should read daily to children and create activities where children discuss stories. Finally, the program must target three goals for learner outcomes: the ability to read independently, the ability to understand and analyze stories, and the development of a positive disposition toward reading. Failure to achieve any of these objectives should lead to a critical review and revision of the program.

Teacher Qualifications

A common false assumption about early childhood teachers is that "the younger the child, the easier the job." This statement could not be more inaccurate in the eyes of those who have studied effective early childhood classrooms. Seefeldt (1985) describes a kindergarten teacher as an active professional who is constantly observing individual children within the group, challenging students to investigate and explore, asking the right questions to help build vocabulary, and encouraging children to develop their skills in problem solving and thinking.

In its survey of state practices, the Public School Early Childhood Study (Mitchell 1987a, 1987b, Marx and Seligson 1987) documents the need for thorough knowledge of early childhood education: About half of those states with early childhood programs require teachers to have early childhood certification, and still more require an early childhood bachelor's degree. The 1985-86 Great City Schools' survey found that prekindergarten teachers employed in 24 of the 28 school districts were on the same salary schedule as the elementary school teachers, and in 27 districts they were required to have a teaching certificate (Schweinhart and Mazur 1987). The National Day Care Study (Ruopp et al. 1979) found that only one teacher characteristic was related to program effectiveness: the amount of early childhood training.

The National Association for the Education of Young Children (NAEYC) has identified training areas. According to NAEYC, teachers in high-quality early childhood programs for 4- and 5-year-olds should have college-level preparation that includes a foundation in child development theory and research, training in developmentally appropriate instructional practices, and supervised field experience with this age group (Bredekamp 1986, NAEYC 1986). Regardless of certification status or academic credentials, teachers should not be in charge of a group of 4- or 5-year-olds until they have had supervised experience teaching that age group according to the field tested accreditation procedures of the National Academy of Early Childhood Programs (NAEYC 1986).

When determining selection qualifications for early childhood teachers in the public schools, administrators must make every effort to ensure that these teachers hold comparable status with other teachers. Candidates should hold a four-year degree and teaching credentials from an accredited higher education institution. It is essential that early childhood teachers have specific training in early childhood education/child development, and supervised practical experiences with young children.

Policy Implications

The expansion of early childhood programs is inevitable in the face of today's social trends and societal needs. Successful expansion will require a delivery system that addresses curriculum design and implementation, teacher preparation, and a comprehensive process for ongoing program analysis, evaluation, and revision. These challenges can be expected to involve policy makers in extended debate, and the accumulation of research and experience in early childhood education should be used to resolve issues and build programs of the highest possible quality.

As state boards of education and local districts compete for tax dollars to maintain existing programs, they will be pressed to make tough decisions about extending the length of the kindergarten day and providing prekindergarten programs for 4-year-olds. In part, the argument for these changes will be driven by the belief that education is strongly related to social and economic development and that financial and societal benefits will accrue for individuals and society through high-quality early childhood education.

While evidence supports the notion that high-quality early childhood education programs have enduring educational effects on young children, the findings are less conclusive with regard to the most appropriate method for delivering the program. The research reveals some important commonalities among programs, such as emphasis on oral language development, high rates of teacher/child interaction, a combination of teacher-led and child-initiated activities, and the need for all children to experience success. Even as educators continue to debate what the optimal combination of teaching/learning approaches may be, there is universal agreement that language development is of utmost importance. This topic permeates the literature and requires the careful attention of policy makers in program planning.

As early childhood programs are expanded to include prekindergartens and extended-day kindergartens, it stands to reason that the elementary school should be adapted to create an optimal continuum of learning. If this ideal is to become a reality, the learning process must be viewed as a fluid, building experience rather than as a series of single experiences that somehow come together to make a whole. The broader school curriculum beginning in prekindergarten and continuing through kindergarten, 1st grade, and beyond should be designed to support a continuous progression of individual development. Transitional grades (e.g., junior or senior kindergartens for children who are not considered ready for the "normal" grade level) are unnecessary within such a framework since learning is individualized and continuous (Shepard and Smith 1986); however, enrichment programs should be available in the summer for all children who want or need them (Brandt 1986).

By definition, programs following developmentally appropriate practice have no place for transitional grades because the curriculum is designed to fit the needs of the individual child. The National Association of Early Childhood Specialists in State Departments of Education (1987) includes transitional classes in its position paper on unacceptable practices in kindergarten entry and placement. This is because

• Transition grades are in effect another name for retention.

• There is no conclusive evidence that retention is effective and experience shows the negative impact of retention on children's self-esteem, social behavior, and attitude toward school.

• The screening devices used to select children for transition grades have questionable reliability and validity, yet they may be the sole criterion for such placement.

Prekindergarten, kindergarten, and other elementary teachers must communicate and plan collaboratively. This is generally not now happening as prekindergarten children come into the public kindergartens from other settings, public or private (Caldwell 1986). Collaboration must include specific attention to the needs of individual children as identified by the other settings.

More than ever, it is important to look at teachers as members of professional teams rather than as isolated teachers of discrete grades or age groups. While recent education proposals call for widespread reform of teacher education, the preparation and education of early childhood teachers who can comprise these teams has not received much attention. A mechanism for enhancing the quality of early childhood education programs is teacher certification or credentials that specify the educational requirements for those who work in programs for young children. The early childhood education community and the research findings on the quality of care share a unanimous recommendation: Teachers of young children must have specific training in early childhood development and education (Grubb 1987).

Once choices are made to establish prekindergarten programs, school officials must develop workable strategies for ongoing program assessment and initiate a self-renewal process for all staff members. In initiating new programs or changing existing ones, it is crucial to provide staff development on a systematic basis for everyone connected with the program. This certainly includes classroom aides and assistants and extends to classified personnel such as cooks, custodians, and bus drivers. This level of commitment can best be attained at the district level by the assignment of personnel whose primary responsibilities are to ensure continuity between educational programs for young children and to provide leadership in developing a coherent, comprehensive process for self-analysis and renewal of the staff and program.

Conclusion

As an area of governmental concern, policies relating to early childhood are still in their infancy. Problems to be resolved seem complex and the choices politically unattractive (e.g., to raise taxes). Still, it is not difficult to see what is good for young children. The research on the effects and quality of early childhood programs along with the years of accumulated experiences with young children provide impetus and information for bringing together high-quality programs for all children. Perhaps then it will be possible to fulfill our belief that all children can learn and become productive adults.

References

Abelson, W., E. Zigler, and C. DeBlasi. "Effects of a Four-Year Follow-Through Program on Economically Disadvantaged Children." *Journal of Educational Psychology* 66 (1974): 750-771.

Barnett, W. Steven. *The Perry Preschool Program and its Long-term Effects: A Benefit-Cost Analysis*. High/Scope Early Childhood Policy Papers, No. 2. Ypsilanti, Mich.: High/Scope Press, 1985.

Brandt, R.S. "On Early Education: A Conversation with Barbara Day." *Educational Leadership* 44, 3 (1986): 28-30.

Bredekamp, Sue. "The Reliability and Validity of the Early Childhood Classroom Observation Scale for Accrediting Early Childhood Programs." *Early Childhood Research Quarterly* 1 (1986): 103-118.

Caldwell, B.M. "Day Care and the Public Schools—Natural Allies, Natural Enemies." *Educational Leadership* 44 (February 1986): 34-39.

Carnegie Forum on Education and the Economy. *A Nation Prepared: Teachers for the 21st Century*. Washington, D.C.: 1985.

Chapman, F.S. "Executive Guilt: Who's Taking Care of the Children?" *Fortune*, February 16, 1987, 30-37.

Coleman, J.S., E.Q. Campbell, C.J. Hobson, J. McPartland, A. Mood, F. Weinfeld, and R. York. *Equality of Opportunity* (FSS-238-38001). Washington, D.C.: U.S. Department of Health, Education, and Welfare, 1966.

Committee for Economic Development. *Children in Need: Investment Strategies for the Educationally Disadvantaged*. New York and Washington: September 1987.

Cowles, Milly. "Four Views of Learning and Development." In *Revisiting Early Childhood Education*, edited by Joe Frost. New York: Holt, Rinehart & Winston, 1974.

Day, Barbara. *Early Childhood Education: Creative Learning Activities*. 3rd ed. New York: Macmillan, 1988.

Day, B.D., and K.N. Drake. *Early Childhood Education: Curriculum Organization and Classroom Management*. Alexandria, Va.: Association for Supervision and Curriculum Development, 1983.

Day, B.D., and K.N. Drake. "Developmental and Experiential Programs: The Key to Quality Care and Education of Young Children." *Educational Leadership* 44, 3 (1986): 25-27.

Durkin, D. "A Six Year Study of Children Who Learned to Read in School at the Age of Four." *Reading Research Quarterly* 1 (1974-75): 50-51.

Engelmann, S., and E. Bruner. *DISTAR Reading Level I*. Chicago: Science Research Associates, 1978.

Engelmann, S., and J. Osborn. *DISTAR Language I*. Chicago: Science Research Associates, 1976.

Gadson, Melvin. *Testing Young Children*. Tallahassee: Florida Department of Education, 1980.

Gallup, A.M. "The 18th Annual Poll of the Public's Attitudes Toward the Public Schools." *Phi Delta Kappan*, September 1986, 43-59.

Gersten, R., D. Carnine, and P. Williams. "Measuring Implementation of a Structured Educational Model in an Urban Setting: An Observational Approach." *Educational Evaluation and Policy Analysis* 4 (1982): 67-69.

Gersten, R., C. Darch, and M. Gleason. "The Effectiveness of Academic Kindergarten for Low-Income Students." *Elementary School Journal*, in press.

Gersten, R., and T. Keating. "Improving High School Performance of 'At

Risk' Students: A Study of Long-term Benefits of Direct Instruction." *Educational Leadership* 44, 6 (1987): 28-31.

Grubb, Norton W. *Young Children Face the States: Issues and Options for Early Childhood Programs.* New Brunswick, N.J.: Center for Policy Research in Education, 1987.

Hanson, R. et al. "Effects on High School Seniors of Learning to Read in Kindergarten." Final Report to the U.S. Department of Education, Grant #8410091, 1987.

Johnson, D.W., and R.T. Johnson. "Student-Student Interaction: Ignored but Powerful." *Journal of Teacher Education* 36, 4 (1985): 22-26.

Leeper, S., R. Witherspoon, and B.D. Day. *Good Schools for Young Children.* 5th ed. New York: Macmillan Publishing Co., 1984.

Marx, F., and M. Seligson. "Draft Notes on States Findings from the Public School Early Childhood Study." Wellesley, Mass.: College Center for Research on Women, 1987.

Meyer, L. "Long-term Academic Effects of the Direct-Instruction Follow Through." *Elementary School Journal* 84 (1984): 380-394.

Mitchell, A. "Public Schools and Young Children: A Report of the First National Survey of Public School Districts Regarding their Early Childhood Programs." Paper prepared for American Education Research Association Annual Meeting, Washington, D.C., April 1987a.

Mitchell, A. "Young Children in Public Schools: Preliminary Results from a National Survey of Public School Districts and Site Visits in Twelve States." New York: Bank Street College Center for Children's Policy, 1987b.

Murray, R. "The Kindergarten Dilemma: Half Day, Full Day, or Every Day." *Catalyst* (1987): 18-21.

Nathan, Joe. "Implications for Educators: Time for Results." *Phi Delta Kappan* (November 1986): 197-201.

National Association for the Education of Young Children. *Developmentally Appropriate Practice.* Washington, D.C., 1986.

National Association for the Education of Young Children. "Where Your Child Care Dollars Go." Washington, D.C.: Author, undated.

National Association of Early Childhood Specialists in State Departments of Education. *Unacceptable Trends in Kindergarten Entry and Placement.* 1987.

National Commission on Excellence in Education. *A Nation at Risk.* Washington, D.C.: 1983.

Pepper, John E. Speech before Leadership-Cincinnati Conference, May 21, 1987, 10-11.

Puleo, V.T. "Current Research Perspective on Full-Day Kindergarten." *ERS Spectrum* (Fall 1986): 32-39.

Robinson, S.L. "Kindergarten in America: Five Major Trends." *Phi Delta Kappan* (March 1987): 529-530.

Ruopp, Richard, Jeff Travers, F. Glantz, and Craig Coelen. *Children at the Center: Summary Findings and Their Implications.* Final Report of the National Day Care Study, Vol. 1. Cambridge, Mass.: Abt Associates, 1979.

Schweinhart, L.J., D.P. Weikart, and M.B. Larner. "Consequences of Three

Preschool Curriculum Models Through Age 15." *Early Childhood Research Quarterly* 1 (1986): 15-45.

Schweinhart, L.J., and Elizabeth Mazur. *Prekindergarten Programs in Public Schools*. High/Scope Early Childhood Policy Papers, No. 6. Ypsilanti, Mich.: High/Scope Press, 1987.

Seefeldt, Carol. "Tomorrow's Kindergarten: Pleasure or Pressure?" *Principal* (May 1985): 12-15.

Shepard, L.A., and M.L. Smith. "Synthesis of Research on School Readiness and Kindergarten Retention." *Educational Leadership* 44, 3 (1986): 78-86.

Zigler, Edward F. "A Solution to the Nation's Child Care Crisis: The School of the Twenty-first Century." Paper presented at the National Health Policy Forum, Washington, D.C., September 1987.

Part II

7
Program Descriptions

CYNTHIA WARGER

Early Childhood Family Education: Minneapolis

Contact: Robert Z. Brancale, Coordinator
Susan Dreves-Libson, Early Childhood Family Education
Specialist
Minneapolis Early Childhood Family Education
1006 West Lake St.
Minneapolis, MN 55408

Background of the Program

Since its inception in 1974, the Minneapolis Early Childhood Family Education (ECFE) program has served thousands of families and their infants, toddlers, and preschool-aged children. During the 1986-87 school year, various components of the Minneapolis ECFE program served 2,525 children aged birth to 6 and their parents. All city residents with young children—regardless of economic status, intellectual range, or at-risk factors—are eligible to participate. Through cooperative partnerships with social service agencies, hospitals, and local government, Minneapolis ECFE has developed programs that addresses the needs of most of the city's young families.

The Minneapolis program began as one of six state pilot programs funded by the Minnesota Legislature and coordinated by the Council on Quality Education. In the original legislation, Senator Jerome Hughes (chief author) identified the child's earliest years as critical to future success in school and life. With other legislators, he created a funding structure for programs that recognize and support the parent as the child's first and most influential teacher.

In 1984, the Minnesota State Legislature created a local levy/ state match funding formula, and Community Education became the administrative and fiscal agent for ECFE programs. Increased funding allowed Minneapolis to expand services by consolidating existing programs geographically.

Currently, Minneapolis has nine regional centers in school district buildings. One program is located in a district special education preschool site and provides services to parents of handicapped and nonhandicapped youngsters. Forty satellite sites in city park buildings, hospitals, social service centers, community buildings, and other locations provide additional ECFE programming and services to families.

Program Mission

ECFE's mission is to build and support the confidence and competence of Minneapolis parents and expectant parents by providing the best possible parent-child interaction and an environment for the social, emotional, physical, and intellectual development of their children, from birth to kindergarten. The ECFE program builds partnerships between the home, the school district, the city and community agencies.

Content of the Program

On the average, families spend two hours a week in classes located at neighborhood ECFE centers. Each week, parents and children participate for 15 to 45 minutes in developmentally appropriate activities in an environment that fosters fun, exploration, and mutual learning. During the remainder of the time, parents go to a parent discussion group and children are cared for in the early childhood room. Parent group participation is voluntary and usually centers on discussion of specific issues (e.g., child development or special interests of the parents). Although support/information groups are predominant, a variety of other models are used to meet the diverse needs of the parents: lecture, guest speakers, videos, and book-focused classes.

As the program has grown, it has been necessary to provide more specialized services. Early childhood teachers and parent educators work closely with special education personnel, social workers, speech clinicians, and physical and occupational therapists to provide screening services or training. The programs are also closely paired to K-12 school programs. Services are provided to expectant teenagers and teen parents. In addition, Minneapolis offers a family-school component for families under severe stress; a parent education component for the school district's special and general education preschoolers, infants and toddlers; topic-based classes on self-esteem and child management; and bilingual classes for southeast Asian and Hispanic parents.

Program Operation

All Minneapolis parents of children aged birth to kindergarten and expectant parents are eligible. In situations where ECFE has a partnership with another agency or with special education, children or parents may have to meet some additional criteria. Although it is not required, all Minneapolis parents are encouraged to participate in formal preschool screening when their child is 3½. A qualified staff member conducts formal screening when a referral to another program has been made.

The program follows the school calendar (September-May). There are two-hour segments during the morning, afternoon, and evening, as well as occasional weekend classes and special events. Presentation techniques and curriculums are designed or modified to meet the specific needs of the community and participants. The ECFE staff members, State Department of Education, local school district, participating parents, and agency representatives all help determine yearly goals for the program.

Community Education, within the Minneapolis Public School District, administers the program. The ECFE Program Coordinator supervises overall program functions and a staff of 84. There are 12 "Teachers on Special Assignment" (TOSA) who are responsible for individual program development, implementation, and support services. TOSA are responsible for designing the program that is implemented by Certified Hourly Teachers (Tutors). All TOSA and Tutors are School District employees who are licensed in the state of Minnesota and hold accredited four-year degrees. Assistant child-care workers complement tutors in the early childhood rooms.

TOSA typically teach two classes a week; tutors teach six to seven classes. For each class session, an early childhood educator and a parent educator are present. The staff/child ratios of 1:3 for infants, 1:7 for toddlers, and 1:12 for preschoolers are maintained for the child's portion of the program.

Program Evaluation

The program is continually evaluated at the state and local levels. Consultants are helping the Minnesota State Department of Education design a longitudinal study to measure long-term program outcomes and impact. ECFE's growth from 6 pilot programs to over 300 programs statewide is probably the most significant indicator of the high degree of parental interest and satisfaction. The confidence of educators and legislators has secured legislative support and funding.

Program Funding

Funds for Early Childhood Family Education come from state and local taxes, parent fees, in-kind contributions from the school district, and grants. The budget for the 1987-88 School Year was approximately $1.8 million. In several cases, TOSA are funded by external agencies.

Unique Element of Program

The Minneapolis Program has undergone dramatic change and growth since 1974. What continues to make it dynamic is the acceptance, involvement, and dedication of educators and helping professionals in providing for the health, growth, and development of the city's children. The fact that ECFE services are available to *all children*; that eligibility is *not* determined by dysfunction; and that the mayor, the city council, the superintendent of schools, the governor of Minnesota, and the state legislature all recognize the importance of early intervention makes Minneapolis an exciting place to be an educator. The coordination of community education, health social service, special education, and K-12 programs provides a global focus and a spirit of cooperation that is unique.

Developmental Placement: St. Charles Parish

Contact: Coy L. Landry, Assistant Superintendent,
Curriculum & Instruction
P. O. Box 46
Luling, LA 70070
(504) 785-6289

Background of the Program

St. Charles Parish is a suburban parish (county) located near New Orleans and divided by the Mississippi River. The total student enrollment in the district is about 8,300. During the 1981-82 school session, two elementary schools, one on each side of the river, piloted the Gesell Screening Instrument, designed to identify a child's developmental level. The schools used the results to place children in educational programs.

Currently, all children who enter school in St. Charles Parish in kindergarten or 1st grade (about 700 a year) are screened for developmental placement. They range in age from 4 years 8 months to 6 years 8 months.

Program Mission

The major goal of the program is to place children in developmentally appropriate early childhood classes that provide curricular experiences designed to meet each child's developmental needs. As a result of placement, children are prepared for the social, emotional, physical, and intellectual challenges of later school years.

Content of Child's Program

Because children develop at different rates, the district offers both developmental kindergarten and kindergarten classes to 5-year-olds. Teachers in the district have developed a curriculum guide (latest revision 1986) for both types of classes. Developmental kindergarten, appropriate for children who are developmentally 4- to 4½-years-old, is structured to allow more movement in a less structured environment. In these classes, teachers identify objectives appropriate for the child's developmental needs and structure a variety of child-centered, experience-based activities. The child's progress is measured through the teacher's observations with the aid of a checklist of developmental tasks.

The kindergarten curriculum is developmentally appropriate

for 5- to 5½-year-old children. The curriculum has a balance of structured and unstructured tasks with both child-directed and teacher-directed activities. Emphasis is on language experiences and hands-on involvement in learning. Student progress is measured through teacher observation and a skills checklist, "Survey of Basic Skills," from Science Research Associates (1985).

Program Operation

Children who are old enough to enter kindergarten and 1st graders who are new to the district are screened to determine their developmental level and school readiness. The Gesell School Readiness Screening Test, developed by the Gesell Institute of Human Development in New Haven, Connecticut, is used to determine initial placement. A review is conducted if teachers' observations and evaluations conflict with this initial placement.

Parental involvement is incorporated into the initial screening stages of the program. In addition, informative meetings are held twice a year at each school with kindergarten students. Under the direction of the classroom teacher, parents serve as information resources, help make manipulatives for the children, chaperone field trips, plan parties, and volunteer in the classroom.

Program Staffing

The supervisor of early childhood education is responsible for the coordination, implementation, and supervision of the program. Principals at each elementary school give direct supervision to guarantee that the program is implemented appropriately. The St. Charles Parish Public School System provides teachers for developmental kindergarten and kindergarten at a ratio of 20 students per teacher. All teachers must be certified as kindergarten teachers by the state of Louisiana and must be trained to administer the Gesell Developmental Assessment. Principals, teachers, and the supervisor of early childhood education meet yearly to revise and evaluate the program.

Program Evaluation

The St. Charles Parish Public School System investigates the effectiveness of developmental placement on overall achievement of young children. Initial findings reveal that by the end of the 1st grade year, children who participate in the developmental program achieve composite SRA scores significantly higher than their peers who were eligible but did not participate in the program. Ongoing research focuses on the long-term effects of developmental placement, specifically on student achievement in reading, language arts, and math; attendance; retention; and social/emotional development.

The program has received state validation as a model program. Approximately 10 other school districts in Louisiana have used the St. Charles model to start similar programs.

Program Funding

Start-up costs for this program, funded by the local school district, included approximately $3,300 for the Gesell consultant to conduct a three-day workshop; $195 per teacher (25) to attend the workshop; $25 for testing kits for each teacher; and $37 for a package of 50 tests.

Kindergarten teachers are funded through the Louisiana State Department of Education allocation, as are regular classroom teachers.

Unique Element of Program

The unique element of our developmental program is that it was initiated by teachers, accepted by their administrators, and wholeheartedly supported by the school board.

Reference

Science Research Associates. *Survey of Basic Skills*. Chicago: 1985.

A Prekindergarten Instructional Television Program: The Brownsville Model

Contact: Emma Gavito, Bilingual Curriculum Coordinator
Brownsville Independent School District
1625 Price Road
Brownsville, TX 78521
(512) 546-5354

Background of the Program

In 1980, statistics showed that 95 percent of the district's kindergarten children would begin their school year speaking little or no English and that the trend would continue. Compounding the problem was the fact that 70 percent of these children came from low-income families. The demographic data, coupled with the results of a districtwide survey, showed an urgent need to develop a preschool model that would prepare students for formal schooling; promote the important influence of parents in their child's school success; and, in so doing, increase the effectiveness of kindergarten teachers.

Faced with the dilemma of designing a preschool program for limited-English-proficient (LEP) children that would involve parents and use limited financial resources, the district opted for an alternative, innovative program that was effective and affordable. In 1980, the federal Office of Bilingual Education and Minority Language Affairs awarded the district a three-year grant to develop El Arco Iris (The Rainbow), a prekindergarten instructional television program.

At the end of the grant period, a decision was made, based on the positive impact of the program on its graduates' performance in kindergarten, to continue funding the program on the 12 original campuses using state and local monies. All principals and kindergarten teachers where the program had been implemented supported this continuation. In 1984-85, all of the district's 24 campuses were implementing the program. By 1986-87, the program included 600 students and their parents, 16 instructional aides, and a program coordinator. The project has produced 36 videotapes with an English and a Spanish lesson. Although this model was designed to meet the needs of a bilingual population, the format is appropriate for school districts that want to involve parents in the education of their children, provide low-cost prekindergarten instruction, and produce their own videotaped lessons.

Program Mission

El Arco Iris is founded on the belief that all children can learn and that all children benefit from an environment that responds to their needs. The district believes that early childhood bilingual programs should:
- Use the learner's native language.
- Provide a firm base for other academic learning experiences.
- Give attention to the physical, social, emotional, and cognitive needs of LEP preschool children.
- Include a learning environment, teaching strategies, and content that responds to the developmental learning needs.
- Employ staff members whose attitudes and behavior reflect an understanding and appreciation of how young children learn.
- Recognize a need to increase the environmental experiences of LEP preschoolers and their parents living in target areas of the community.
- Promote maximum language development in both English and Spanish.

El Arco Iris was designed to upgrade the entrance level readiness skills of prekindergarten LEP children. The general goals center on four skill areas: cognitive, physical, social/emotional and language development.

Program Operation

El Arco Iris incorporates instructional television into the child's daily lessons. In developing the lessons, an assumption was made that preschoolers learn concepts primarily through direct, personal experience. Thus, television supplements actual face-to-face lessons with children and their parents.

Parental participation is mandated. If a parent or relative does not attend the class, the child cannot participate. Two 1½-hour sessions are offered each week. First, parents and children view major parts of the instructional videotape together. Following the tape, they are grouped separately with two instructional aides. The children's aide reinforces the objectives of the lesson, and the parents' aide discusses the lesson and demonstrates at-home enrichment activities. Parents are coached on how they can improve their children's academic achievement and self-concept at home.

The children's lessons were derived from many sources including the *Bilingual Early Childhood Program Level Two* by the Southwest

Educational Development Laboratory (SEDL) of Austin, Texas, and the *Peabody Early Experiences Kit (PEEK)*. The SEDL program was selected because it was developed for preschool children, written in both Spanish and English, and met many of the program goals and objectives. PEEK was also developed for preschool age children, met the many goals and objectives of the project, and had many bright, attractive teaching pictures.

Each videotape contains a lesson, storytelling segment, and home activity. Each videotape lesson generally covers some aspect of visual and auditory skill development and contains such elements as field trips, puppets, and characters. Videotaped field trips are designed to broaden the children's experiences while increasing their vocabulary. Puppets and characters are used for developing expression, enhancing communication skills, and reinforcing concepts. The main goal of the storytelling component is to help the children learn to listen; a secondary goal is to enable them to sequence ideas, increase vocabulary, and enlarge their experiential background. The home activity component provides the children with opportunities to develop fine motor skills and review newly learned concepts.

The videotape themes focus on the child, family, and the community. Many holiday themes are introduced as a way to help the child learn about the cultural context of the community.

The total program can be implemented at any school location (classroom, library, cafeteria) where chairs and two or three tables are available for 90 consecutive minutes. A videocassette recorder and color television are needed in addition to typical classroom materials such as scissors, crayons, construction paper, and glue. Twenty-six videotape lessons have been developed for the program.

Program Evaluation

Student achievement gains are determined through pre/post test results on the Cooperative Preschool Inventory (CPI), which assesses language development and general cognitive skills and concepts among 3- to 5-year-olds. Both English and Spanish versions of the CPI may be administered. Results are compared against the norm group or gains of a group of nonparticipating students in the district.

The average attendance of El Arco Iris students from 1980-84 ranged from 58 to 70 hours each school year. Students with more than 12 hours of instruction improved significantly in both English and Spanish reading readiness. Program graduates who have completed 1st and 2nd grade average higher normal curve equivalent levels in reading and math than other students in their home school and districtwide. Figure 7.1 shows results of the Comprehensive Tests of Basic Skills (CTBS) administered in English.

On a questionnaire administered to parents, 100 percent of the respondents stated that they were satisfied with the services of the project, 70 percent stated that their children's English usage had improved, and 100 percent stated that they were pleased with their children's level of academic progress.

In 1985, El Arco Iris was validated as an exemplary program and selected for the Demonstration Programs for School Improvement Network by the Texas Education Agency.

Figure 7.1

Follow-Up Data for 1981-82 Graduates, N = 74

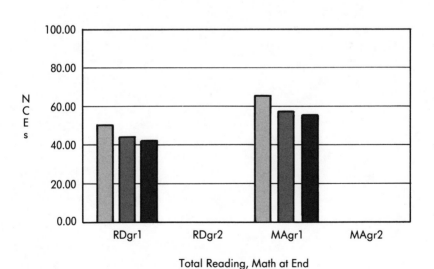

Total Reading, Math at End
Of Grade 1

Program Funding

The program, excluding videotape development costs, is approximately $300 per student. A new adoption site could expect to budget $50 per lesson for the cost of reproducing videotapes and materials and $300 per student to pay for staff and support personnel. The more teams in a district, the lower the cost per pupil since only one coordinator is needed for any number of teams. Districts may also opt to use only the children's lessons or only the parent's lessons.

Visitors to the various program sites are welcome by appointment. The program may be modified by school districts offering daily preschool and summer school programs.

Most Significant Feature of Program

El Arco Iris combines educational techniques with technology (instructional television) to create an effective teaching tool, emphasizes parents' importance and support in the early education of children, enables school districts to offer a preschool program without sacrificing a teacher or classroom, and demonstrates to school districts how to create their own videotape lessons.

Public School Montessori Program: Dallas

Contact: Andrew D. Martin Ed.D., Principal
L.L. Hotchkiss Montessori Academy
Dallas Independent School District
6929 Town North Dr.
Dallas, TX 75230
(214) 348-3730

Background of the Program

The Dallas public school Montessori Program was established in 1976 to comply with a federal desegregation order. Housed at Amelia Earhart Elementary School, which also ran a traditional program, the Montessori program began with 100 4th and 5th graders in 5 classrooms. In 1978, another classroom for 1st, 2nd, and 3rd graders was added to offer the Montessori experience to more children coming into the upper-grade program. And in 1981, the first classroom for 5-year-olds was opened.

The program moved to L.L. Hotchkiss School in 1984. This was a total Montesssori campus with two kindergarten units, 9 grade 1-3 units, 10 grade 4-6 units, and 4 grade 7-8 (500 students). With the addition of 2 more grade 7-8 units, the program now serves 550 students.

Program Goal

The major goal of the Montessori program is to prepare children for life. Montessori is a philosophy, methodology, and curriculum premised on the idea that children have "absorbent minds" and an innate desire to learn. Given the proper environment and freedom, children will direct their own learning activities.

Content of Child's Program

Learning is by self-discovery. The Montessori method places the responsibility for learning on the student, who actually learns from the environment, not from the teacher. The teacher is a dynamic link between the class environment and the student, and it is through this link that learning takes place.

The use of special Montessori equipment is a key feature of the L.L. Hotchkiss Montessori Academy. Through manipulation of such materials as a geometric cabinet and grammar boxes, students learn not only the fundamentals of mathematics, language arts, social studies, and science, but also how to combine facts and arrange data in new and exciting ways. Additional subject areas include geometry, preparation for algebra, botany, zoology, computers, astronomy, ecology, and the history of man. The Suzuki Strings program, piano, art, and physical education are all provided by certified teachers in each area.

The child must master each unit of study before moving on. Mastery is noted by visual, oral, or written evaluations that depend upon the exercise being evaluated. Large units of subject evaluations are seldom used.

Program Operation

District students who want the special emphasis available at this Montessori school are eligible. The student must be:
- in the 50th percentile or greater on standardized tests in reading and mathematics
- able to receive instruction and follow through independently with self-control
- recommended by the sending school/teacher
- accepted through parental and student interviews.

Students who meet these criteria are accepted based on the date of receipt of the application and within court ethnic guidelines: 40 percent black, 20 percent Latin American, 40 percent other.

Transportation is provided by district school buses where 20 or more students live close together and request it. School classes begin at 8:15 A.M. and end at 3:15 P.M.

A large number of parents are active in the Parent Teacher Association. Parents who are new to Montessori education are encouraged to attend parent education meetings on the Montessori method, philosophy, and curriculum.

Since the educational program at L.L. Hotchkiss is a public school program, it is administered and supervised like any other state program. Staff members must meet all state accreditation and certification requirements; all classroom teachers and principals are also Montessori certified.

Program Evaluation

Program evaluation at Hotchkiss is ongoing; the state and district grade-level curriculum standards are tested regularly. Students' average scores are consistently in the top 10 percent of the district schools.

Unique Feature of the Program

The Montessori classroom environment is the unique element of the program. It fosters students' independence and personal responsibility for learning, willingness to take risks, sense of social responsibility, and love for learning.

Child Development Program: Pomona

Contact: Bill Ewing, Administrator
Pomona Unified School District
153 East Pasadena St.
Pomona, CA 91767
(714) 623-1461

Background of the Program

The first Children's Center in Pomona was established in 1969. Today, Pomona's Child Development Program provides child care and development services in a variety of settings to approximately 900 children aged 6 weeks to 14 years.

Head Start and State Preschool programs are comprehensive prekindergarten programs that operate part day using the High/Scope curriculum. Parent involvement is emphasized.

School Age Parenting Infant Development program provides child care to the infants and toddlers of school-age parents who are completing their education. This program also provides funds to teach parenting skills to both parents and nonparents.

Children's Centers provide year round child care/development services to the infants, toddlers, preschool, and school-age children of parents who are working or in training. These services are offered during the day, the evening, and on weekends. Services are also offered to the mildly ill child. Families are eligible for Children's Centers based on their income and pay fees on a sliding scale. The High/Scope curriculum is used at the centers.

School Age Community Care Services is a program for "latchkey" children and is now a part of the School Age Child Care program of the District. Fees are on a sliding scale to eligible families; others pay full cost.

The Child Care Food Program provides breakfast, lunch, supper, and meal supplements to the Child Development Programs.

Resource and Referral provides child care information and assistance throughout a wide geographical area.

Child Protective Services or Respite provides limited-term child care to families of any income level who are under stress. This is provided through a system of subcontracts with licensed group centers and licensed family day-care homes.

Alternative Paymentis a program that provides continuing child care/development services to eligible families on a sliding fee scale basis. These services are provided through a network of licensed family day-care homes and licensed group centers.

Program Mission

The purpose of the program is to provide quality child care/development services so that parents can become or remain self-sufficient.

Content of Child's Program

Pomona adopted the High/Scope Curriculum model (Hohmann et al. 1978). The implementation of the curriculum is coordinated by a member of the staff who is a High/Scope trainer. Teachers use instructional approaches recommended by the High/Scope Curriculum. Child progress is measured by a local instrument.

Eligibility is defined by state and/or federal requirements. Formal testing occurs only in Head Start.

This year-round program operates seven days a week, with child care services offered as early as 6:00 A.M. and as late as midnight. Part-day programs such as Head Start and State Preschool operate 175 days each year. Parents are involved as advisers to and as participants in the classroom.

Administration and Supervision of the Program

The program is administered by a full-time administrator, a coordinator, and a program assistant. At schools, the principal is included in the supervision of Head Start personnel.

Each Child Care/Development Center is directed by a head teacher. Other staff members include teachers who must hold an appropriate teaching permit issued by the state and instructional aides. The program also has one full-time and one part-time nurse, one part-time licensed psychologist, and clerical and custodial staff.

Program Evaluation

The program is subject to an annual quality review. This is a self-review that measures all aspects of the program. In addition, the state participates in the review process every third year. Quality review is ongoing.

California has used the Pomona program as a model for infant care. It was 1 of 13 public school prekindergarten programs selected by Bank Street College for a national study.

Program Funding

Except for Head Start, all funds come from the California State Department of Education and from parent fees.

Alternative Payment Child Care	190,028
General Child Development	1,622,440
Head Start/State Preschool	404,829
State Preschool	146,463
Respite	22,866
Resource and Referral	104,488
School-Age Parenting Infant Development	116,363
Latchkey	57,074
School-Age Child Care, Parent Supported	104,151
Child Care Food Program	180,000
Local—Parent Fees, Interest, Other	54,000
Total	**3,002,702**

Unique Element of the Program

The program is diverse. It operates seven days a week, year round, with services as early as 6:00 A.M. and as late as midnight. There is a program for children who are mildly ill. There is also a resource and referral component that is a part of the state's Resource and Referral Program. Short-term child care is available for parents under stress. The School Age Parenting Infant Development Program permits students who are parents to complete their high school education.

Reference

Hohmann, M., B. Banet, and D. Weikart. *Young Children in Action*. Ypsilanti, Mich.: High/Scope Press, 1978.

Large Urban District: The District of Columbia Model

Contact: Constance C. Mair, Supervising Director
District of Columbia Public Schools, Early Childhood
Kenilworth Elementary School
44th & Nash Sts., N.E.
Washington, DC 20019
(202) 724-4528

Background of the Program

Beginning as early as 1898, Washington, D.C., Public Schools (DCPS) have supported early childhood education with public kindergarten. Full-day preschool centers for 3- and 4-year-olds were established by DCPS in 1964 through an experimental model school system. The pre-K program was widely implemented by 1968. Three years before the passage of PL 94-142 (the Education for All Handicapped Children Act of 1975), DCPS was providing center- and home-based programs for developmentally delayed 4- and 5-year-olds. Early special educational programs for 3-year-olds was extended after 1975. In response to the needs of teen parents, DCPS opened an infant/toddler center in a public high school in 1981. Expansion of this program to three additional high schools was planned for the 1987-88 school year.

Approximately 11,000 children from 6 weeks through 5 years of age are currently served through early childhood programs in DCPS. At-risk infants of low SES teen parents and children eligible for Head Start are included in the student population, along with 3,500 4-year-olds enrolled in 174 prekindergarten classes and 6,600 kindergartners in 283 classes in the 120 public elementary schools. DCPS is truly unique in both its historic and widespread support of early education experiences for its children.

Goal of Program

The goals of the DCPS Early Childhood Program include:
• Building upon the knowledge, strength, and life experiences that children bring to school.
• Providing for the development of the whole child.
• Ensuring a healthy, safe, and secure environment that provides optimal learning.
• Promoting parent-professional partnerships for effective early childhood education.

• Providing a professional development program for staff to enhance and promote the knowledge, skills, and competencies required to implement the goals and objectives of the early childhood programs.

The program aims to provide educational experiences that respect the individual growth and cultural patterns of children from birth to 5 years of age with equal attention and care given to their emotional, physical, intellectual, and social development.

Content of Child's Program

Consistent with the DCPS competency-based curriculum approach to education, prekindergarten and kindergarten curriculum guides contain specific sequenced objectives that provide teachers with organized monthly units designed to integrate skills. The curriculum emphasizes development across physical, social, emotional, and intellectual areas, and learning centers provide a selection of activities for children. Classrooms differ in the degree of teacher- and child-initiated activities. Student progress is measured by observation techniques; curriculum guides give teachers descriptions of what to look for as children respond to activities. Progress records are maintained for each child, and each school has the services of a school counselor who consults with the speech therapist, school psychologist, nutritionists, or nurse in special cases.

Operational Details of the Program

Children who turn 4 or 5 by December 31 of the school year are eligible for prekindergarten or kindergarten respectively. At the time of enrollment, parents must present the child's birth certificate, proof of residency, record of immunizations, and completed medical and dental evaluation forms. Prekindergarten students are enrolled on a space-available basis. Kindergarten-aged children are given priority in the enrollment process, and their neighborhood schools are required to accommodate all who wish to enroll.

Class sizes are set at 20 for kindergartners and prekindergartners with a teacher and an aide. All prekindergarten and kindergarten students attend all day (9:00 A.M.-3:00 P.M.). The Metropolitan Readiness Test is administered to kindergarten children in October; prekindergarten teachers are required to complete the prekindergarten Observational Checklist for each child by the end of November.

Parents are necessary partners in the early childhood program.

They are required to attend parent conferences, are encouraged to participate in self-selected activities, and are informed regularly of the program through a monthly parent calendar, classroom visits, notes, and telephone calls.

Administration and Supervision of the Program

Early childhood programs in DCPS are administered by four regional assistant superintendents who are responsible for all programs in schools within their regions. Principals are responsible to the regional superintendents and for the supervision and implementation of the early childhood program in their schools. Each of the four regions has a support staff to assist the local schools. The Early Childhood Office coordinates all of the programs.

Program Staffing

All teachers of prekindergarten children must be college graduates and meet the prekindergarten/kindergarten certification requirements. Kindergarten teachers are generally certified as elementary school teachers (K-6). Many of them, however, have prekindergarten/kindergarten certification.

Program Evaluation

A preliminary evaluation of DCPS pre-K programs in 1969 indicated that as a result of early educational experiences, children improved primarily in the use of language. Research begun in 1987 will determine differential program effectiveness, short- and long-term influences of pre-K on overall development, and the impact of environmental factors on school competence. As three successive cohorts of pre-K and at-risk children are followed through DCPS, comparisons with the performance of children lacking pre-K experience will indicate the effect of early education on our urban school system. Program quality (using the guidelines of the National Association for the Education of Young Children and the Southern Association of Children Under Six) is being monitored, as well as the extent to which goals of pre-K programs are understood and accepted at the local school level.

Students, educators, and other citizens responded positively to a 1987 survey of their perceptions of the program.

Program Funding

Approximately $12 million from regular appropriated funds support the strongest elements of the program. Additional funds are available through social services agencies, federal funds for Head Start, and private foundations.

Strongest Element of the Program

Community and administrative support, as well as the three-year evaluation study, are the strongest elements of the program.

Early Prevention of School Failure:
A Nationally Validated Program

Contact: Luceille Werner, National Program Director
Curriculum Services
114 North Second St.
Peotone, IL 60468
(312) 258-3478

Background of the Program

The Early Prevention of School Failure Program (EPSF) was originally developed and field tested from 1971-1974 in 13 school districts located in Will and Kankakee Counties of northeastern Illinois. Currently, the program serves over 50,000 young children identified as being at risk in preschool, kindergarten, and 1st grade classes throughout the United States, Canada, and Virgin Islands.

Program Mission

Each child's developmental level in language, auditory, visual, and motor skills and preferred learning style is identified. Based on this diagnosis, the program provides classroom teachers, specialists, and parents with effective teaching strategies and curriculum resources to meet the educational needs of at-risk students.

Program Operation

To determine each child's developmental level and preferred learning style, all 4-, 5-, and 6-year-old children are screened with five validated instruments, a parent interview form, and an observation scale. From this information, it is determined whether the child is functioning more than one year below his or her chronological age in language, auditory, visual, or motor skills. A child found to be functioning below level becomes eligible to receive 15 to 20 minutes of special programming daily.

Children who score in the moderate or considerable need areas in language, visual, auditory, fine motor, and gross motor are grouped for instruction. The teacher plans 10- to 20-minute lessons per week for each modality area. A variety of resource materials in the concrete, semi-concrete, and abstract areas are provided for the teacher to effectively teach the 52 pre-academic skills necessary for future success. A curriculum guide and many activity guides are available.

Parents have several opportunities to be actively involved in the program. In addition to providing teachers with suggestions for helping their own child, they may work in the classroom and meet with other parents to discuss ways of helping all children achieve school success.

Administration and Supervision of the Program

The building principal is the important educational leader in implementing this program. The principal is encouraged to participate in the initial two-day inservice program, assist with parent orientation, and monitor the ongoing program.

The EPSF Program is implemented in the regular classroom by preschool, kindergarten, or 1st grade teachers with support from specialists and parents. Before instructing in the program, teachers receive two days of inservice training on how to administer the five screening instruments, use the computer program, and provide direct modality instruction for at risk students. Special education, Chapter I, and physical education staff members may also be involved.

Program Evaluation

Annual reviews and several ongoing longitudinal studies provide evidence that the program works. New schools that become involved in the program must agree to submit pre- and post-test data collection the first year they use the program.

This nationally validated program has received much recognition and approval since the first national validation in 1974. Recent recognition includes National Re-Certification, 1984, and recognition by the U.S. Office of Education and by numerous states, 1984-87, as an effective "program to address the 'at-risk' students." Awards include the Educational Pacesetter Award presented by the President's National Advisory Council on Supplementary Centers and Services, 1973; United States Office of Education for Outstanding Education Contribution to ESEA, Title I/NDN, 1978; and Recognition as an Outstanding National Migrant Program, 1986.

Program Funding

The EPSF Program is funded by the U.S. Office of Education for dissemination to other schools through the National Diffusion Network. In addition, selected states have identified that the EPSF Nationally Validated Program qualifies for funding through Chapter

II, Chapter I, Bilingual, Special Education, Gifted, At Risk, and Migrant monies. The California Legislature has funded the program since 1985 at over $400,000 yearly.

Unique Element of the Program

The nationally validated program continues to produce documentation that it works for children in all types of settings and where English may be a child's second language. The program is committed to maintaining high expectations for the achievement of all students regardless of family background or social class.

The Integrated Kindergarten Program: Fairfax County

Contact: Dolores Varnon, Principal
Westbriar Elementary
1741 Pine Valley Dr.
Vienna, VA 22180

Background of the Program

In response to teachers' and principals' concerns about the proliferation of curriculum content, instructional objectives, and materials in the elementary school, Fairfax County Public Schools took on the task of integrating the curriculum into a sound, balanced, manageable instructional program beginning with kindergarten. This project was initiated by the district's Department of Instructional Services in February 1984. Teachers, principals, and curriculum specialists identified the instructional needs of young children, as well as the curriculum content and learning processes that would best address the children's needs.

Currently, the program serves 9,750 students, 4½ to 5½-years-old, who are in kindergarten and selected special education classes. The curriculum incorporates "response lessons" for identifying and challenging potentially gifted students.

Program Mission

The major goal of the Integrated Kindergarten Program is to provide a sound, balanced instructional program that integrates learning for young children. It incorporates the content and process objectives from *all* subject areas and allows teachers to meet the social, emotional, physical, and intellectual needs of children in their classrooms. Through participation in the curriculum, children have learning experiences that enable them to communicate orally; interact with others; solve problems; think critically; inquire; observe; create; and develop concepts for reading, writing, and computation.

Content of Child's Program

The Integrated Kindergarten Program is designed to provide students with a sound foundation for future learning. The focus is on the child as an active learner; the curriculum is designed and implemented to emphasize the process of learning.

The kindergarten curriculum is organized into three major instructional strands: integrated language arts, mathematics/science, and music/movement.

Integrated Language Arts Strand. This strand provides 10 thematic units of study that incorporate content and objectives from the language arts, social studies, environmental science, art, and health. The units—Names and Address, All About Me, Working Together, Families, Foods, Senses, Weather/Seasons, Mapping, Plants, and Animals—provide many integrated, activity-oriented experiences. Children are continually involved in oral communication, including listening and speaking; reading; and writing. The suggested broad and open-ended learning experiences allow all children to experience success at their own developmental level.

Mathematics—Science Strand. This strand provides experiences in the areas of mathematics and physical science. Objectives, inquiry experiences, and manipulative materials are organized into six instructional units. Units such as Free Exploration, Sorting and Classifying, Number Concepts, Patterns, Comparing, and Number Experiments are presented to children in a manner that promotes the basic understanding of mathematics and science concepts before requiring children to work with abstract symbols. Manipulative materials for mathematics and equipment to organize and store these materials have been provided to every kindergarten teacher in Fairfax county.

Music—Movement Strand. The music/movement strand integrates content and objectives to provide learning experiences in the areas of music and physical education. Children are involved in activities that emphasize the development of perceptual-motor skills, physical fitness, coordination, musical skills, and creative expression.

Operational Details of the Program

The Integrated Kindergarten Program is used in all kindergarten and designated special education classes for young children in Fairfax County Public Schools. A three-part evaluation package has been developed and was being piloted in select schools during the 1987-88 school year. This package consists of an initial assessment instrument, a curriculum checklist for teachers, and a report card.

Parent education is an essential component of the program. Materials have been developed for principals and teachers to use with parents in orientation and open-house sessions. They include transparencies with a script that gives an overview of the program and six videotapes that address subjects such as readiness for kindergarten, curriculum, and play theory. Teachers are also provided with parent materials that explain the program and provide activities for home learning.

Staff Development for the Program

Strong staff development assured successful implementation of the curriculum. Workshops were held during contracted time and substitute coverage was provided. Additionally, the workshops were planned and conducted by kindergarten teachers and curriculum specialists. The workshops were spaced so that teachers could try out the language arts strategies with their classes before they returned for the next workshop. Teachers were directly involved in classroom observations, sharing, coaching, and feedback.

Program Evaluation

Teachers were involved in all stages of developing, implementing, and evaluating this program. Groups of elementary school principals also reviewed curriculum materials and were asked for recommendations. In addition to field testing the program in 8 elementary schools, the curriculum materials were distributed to 287 kindergarten teachers and stamped "draft." In so doing, all kindergarten teachers in Fairfax County Public Schools had an opportunity to use, evaluate, and suggest revisions before the program was finalized.

Evaluations by teachers indicate that the Integrated Kindergarten Program has:
• eliminated curriculum overlap
• simplified planning for instruction
• infused effective curriculum research on oral language development, reading, writing, and mathematics into the program
• provided a manageable, objective-based instructional program that is sound, balanced, and integrates learning for young children. Metropolitan Readiness Test scores are being monitored.

Program Funding

Staff and Curriculum Development	$41,000 for 2 years
Student Materials	$15 per student
Students Served	9,750
Teachers Involved	287

Strongest Element of Program

The program was the result of a collaborative effort by many knowledgeable, creative, and caring educators determined to provide ways of pulling subject areas and learning processes into a manageable, child-oriented curriculum.

The curriculum project:

• responded to the concerns of teachers

• was conceptually sound and based on research and experience

• was created, tested, and revised by teachers

• provided a staff development program that actively involved teachers in classroom observations, coaching, and feedback sessions

• provided teachers with lesson materials, manipulatives, furniture, and techniques for managing instruction

• provided ongoing support to teachers through newsletters, staff visits, inservice training sessions, parent education programs.

Pre-1st Grade: Broward County

Contact: Linda W. Coffey, Director
Early Childhood Education
School Board of Broward County, Florida
1739 N.E. 13 St.
Fort Lauderdale, FL 33304
(305) 765-6363

Background of the Program

This program was established in Broward County, Florida, as a pilot program in 10 elementary schools in the 1981-82 school year. Five schools were experimental, and five were control schools. Since that time the program has expanded to include all 100 elementary schools.

The Broward County Public School System currently serves approximately 2,000 pre-1st grade students each school year. Pre-1st grade students are required by Florida Statute to be 5 years old on or before September 1 of the kindergarten entry year. Students who participate in the pre-1st program are those who need additional readiness before the formal structure of 1st grade.

Program Mission

The major goal of the program is to provide curricular expectations and outcomes compatible with classroom activities relevant to the student's intellectual, social, emotional, and physical growth and development.

Overview of Program

Students who have satisfactorily completed kindergarten but who are not yet ready for the formal reading program of 1st grade are eligible for pre-1st grade placement. Parents have the option of electing pre-1st or 1st grade placement.

The student's kindergarten program is a diagnostic-prescriptive year. The program is served by the school staff and an interdisciplinary team (consisting of a psychologist, speech clinician, audiologist, social worker, educational specialist, and team leader). The screening program includes both a health and an educational component and provides numerous screening and follow-up measures.

The pre-1st grade is a full-day, year-round program. Parents are encouraged to attend seminars offered during the spring of the kindergarten year, to visit classrooms, and to volunteer their services.

The pre-1st grade curriculum emphasizes language experiences. Teaching strategies focus on exploration and discovery through interdisciplinary experiences. Two programs, *Language Experiences In Reading*, published by Encyclopaedia Britannica Educational Corporation, and *Happily Ever After*, published by Addison-Wesley Publishing Company, are used.

Student progress is measured by classroom observation and program objective tests that include the mastery of minimum basic skills. Teachers of pre-1st grade students hold conferences with parents rather than send home a written report card, and students are exempted from the countywide test program until the end of the 1st grade.

The program is administered and supervised by the elementary school principal and primary specialist. Each classroom is staffed by a certified teacher and teacher aide.

Program Evaluation

Evaluation studies have established that students who attend pre-1st classes are more popular than those whose parents rejected the recommended pre-1st option and entered their children directly into 1st grade. Developmental maturity, as measured by the Gesell School Readiness Screening Test, was significantly associated with future success on achievement tests. In addition, decisions about placement into the pre-1st grade program were based primarily on academic readiness rather than Gesell results.

A 1987 evaluation followed up on students who entered the 1st grade during the 1982-83, 1983-84, 1984-85, and 1985-86 school years. Each group was divided into four levels:
- students who attended pre-1st grade
- students whose parents rejected pre-1st placement
- regular 1st grade students
- students who failed kindergarten

Withdrawal, failure rates, and achievement test results indicated that placement in a pre-1st program was not a significant factor in determining whether students remained in school. However, students who attended pre-1st classes had the lowest failure rate.

In addition, the findings showed that pre-1st graders obtained better achievement test results in terms of their ability than did those whose parents opted for 1st rather than pre-1st grade. The establishment of the pre-1st programs has made a positive impact upon student achievement in the county.

The Broward County Pre-1st Grade was featured on Dan Rather's CBS evening news in December, 1985, as well as in numerous newspapers and magazines.

Program Funding

This program is funded like all program in Florida. The funding formula is based on full-time equivalency. No additional funds support the program; rather, it is a reorganization of the primary grade structure.

Program Strengths

The two strongest outcomes of the program, as identified by the longitudinal study, show that:

• Students who attend pre-1st grade become more popular, self-assured, and develop a high degree of self-worth.

• Pre-1st grade students obtain higher test scores in terms of their ability than their peers who rejected the pre-1st grade option.

Integrating Special Needs Learners into Mainstream Classrooms: Westside Community Schools

Contact: Penny Gildea, Director of Early Childhood Education
Doreen Schelle, Special Education Teacher
Westside Community Schools and
Westside Early Childhood Centers
909 South 76th St.
Omaha, NE 68114
(402) 390-2100 or (402) 390-8205

Background of the Program

The Westside Community Schools established a program of early childhood education in 1968 to examine the significance of early childhood years for subsequent education, and to determine the role the public school should assume in early education and development of children.

The first preschool was housed in a portable unit. In 1977, the program expanded to include a day-care component to serve children whose parents worked outside of the home. In August 1977, a preschool was opened at another elementary school, and the care component was added in 1982. Since 1982, preschools with a care component have been established in four schools. A toddler program was added in the fall of 1987.

Westside Early Childhood Centers had a total enrollment of 478 children for the school year 1987-88, with 15 toddlers (18 months to 3 years old), 253 preschoolers (3 to 5 years old), 174 school-aged children (5 to 12 years old), and 36 special needs children.

The children represent the total spectrum of learning styles, abilities, and special needs (e.g., mentally handicapped, multi-handicapped, orthopedically impaired, speech-language impaired, hearing impaired, and other health impaired).

Program Mission

The major goal is to provide high-quality education and care for children year-round. This includes toddler care, preschool education, preschool day care, and before school and afterschool care encompassing children from 18 months to 12 years.

The goal for the special needs component is to provide a least restrictive environment for the handicapped child. The majority of children are cared for in a totally integrated learning environment.

Westside Early Childhood Centers believe in the philosophy of learning through play. Daily lesson plans reflect the High/Scope philosophy and curriculum.

Overview of the Program

Program eligibility is defined by the guidelines of Nebraska's Rule 51 (1987). A Multi Disciplinary Team uses several formal tests to determine the handicapping conditions of the child. Multi Disciplinary Team members are a school psychologist, speech therapist, occupational therapist, physical therapist, vision specialist, hearing specialist, or an educational diagnostician.

Children are placed in one of the district's six Early Childhood Centers. In four of the centers, speech- and language-delayed children are mainstreamed. One center serves all mainstreamed special-needs preschoolers.

A typical day at Westbrook Early Childhood Center where the special needs preschooler is mainstreamed follows this general schedule.

7 A.M.-9 A.M.	Before school care
9 A.M.-11:30 A.M.	Preschool (special needs children mainstreamed)
11:30A.M.-12:15 P.M.	Lunch; Feeding program for severely/profoundly handicapped children
12:15 P.M.-6:00 P.M.	After school care
1:00 P.M.-3:30 P.M.	Special needs preschool with some mainstreaming in day-care

The curriculum is implemented through the High/Scope philosophy and techniques (Hohmann et al. 1978). Specially designed materials and activities help develop skills and concepts through directed and free play periods. Children are encouraged to be independent and experiment with their environment. They are allowed to use their senses to learn about the world around them.

Hands-on, active learning is carried out in all instructional approaches. Children experience active learning, language, representation, classification, seriation, number concepts, spatial relations, time, and movement.

There is an open door policy for parents at all of the centers. Parents are encouraged to visit, volunteer, provide snacks, or be a story teller. Parents are informed of the concepts and activities that the children are working on and encouraged to share their own resources with the preschool program.

The parents and teachers have organized the Parent Advisory Committee (PAC). Through PAC they share in policy making, discuss problems, and conduct special projects.

Program Staffing

Programs are staffed with the following ratios:

Toddlers (18 months-3 years)	1:5
3-year-olds	1:8
Preschool	1:10
School-age	1:10-1:15

The director must have a Masters in either Early Childhood Education or Elementary Education or a Bachelors Degree plus 36 hours in Child Development or Early Childhood. Head Teachers, who administer the programs, are required to have a Bachelors Degree in Elementary Education with a Child Development or Early Childhood Endorsement and hold a valid Nebraska State Teaching Certificate.

Lead teachers must have a Bachelors Degree in Elementary Education or a related field. Their responsibilities include making plans, organizing and leading activities for children in the center, supervising assistant teachers, and working cooperatively with parents and staff. Special needs teachers must have a degree in Special Education and a valid Nebraska State Teaching Certificate.

Each center also has assistant teachers, clerical aides, and student aides who supervise children in activities, direct children in eating and toileting, and help in the upkeep of the center.

The program is administered by the supervising principal and director of Early Childhood Centers, who work closely with the head teacher and the department head of special education. Each of the head teachers is directly responsible for the supervision of the lead teachers, assistant teachers, clerical aides, and student aides under them.

Recognition of the Program

The Westside Early Childhood Centers were 1 of 12 programs across the nation chosen for a national study on exemplary public school programs conducted by Bank Street College.

Program Funding

The six Early Childhood Centers are conducted through the Westside Community Schools Foundation, Inc., a non-profit, tax-exempt organization incorporated in 1975.

Funding sources are:
- *Local.* (District 66) Building space, utilities, custodial services, administrative time and transportation.
- *State/Federal.* Preschool handicapped (special education pays tuition for mainstreaming).
- *Parent Advisory Council.* Emergency tuition fund, fund raisers.
- *Tuition/Parent Fees.* Major revenue.

Tuition costs are determined by number of days served (two to five per week) and whether the child participates in extended day-care programs.

Strongest Program Element

The length of time that the Westside Education Childhood Centers have been operating is in itself a unique factor. But, the strongest factor of the program is the mainstreaming of the special needs children into the regular education preschool. Through daily interaction, regular education children learn to accept and understand human differences. Regular education children serve as age appropriate role models for the special needs learners.

References

Hohmann, M., B. Banet, and D. Weikart. *Young Children in Action.* Ypsilatni, Mich.: High/Scope Press, 1978.
Nebraska Department of Education. Rule 51. Regulations and Standards for Special Education Programs. Title 92, Nebraska Administrative Code-Chapter 51

Developmental/Experiential K-1
Early Childhood Program:
Chapel Hill

Contact: Barbara Lawler, Principal
Kay Drake, Markie Pringle, Teachers
Seawell Elementary School
Seawell School Rd.
Chapel Hill, NC 27514
(919) 967-4343

Background of the Program

The Chapel Hill program at Seawell Elementary School serves 52 5- and 6-year-old children in a public school setting. Seawell was built in 1970, and the developmental early childhood program has been in place since that time. Children who attend the school live in its attendance area and come from diverse ethnic and socioeconomic backgrounds. Children are grouped heterogeneously, and a wide range of intellectual levels is served. Educationally handicapped children are typically mainstreamed into this program.

Program Mission

The major goal of this program has been to translate developmental theory into appropriate educational practice for young children. Four basic guidelines have been drawn from the large body of developmental research (Bloom 1981; Carroll 1963; Elkind 1986; Piaget 1952):
• Early childhood education should focus on the *total* child, taking into consideration the cognitive, affective, and psychomotor growth of the child.
• The curriculum must be organized around the developmental needs, interests, and learning styles of each child, rather than around a single test, curriculum guide, or time schedule.
• The learning environment must encourage each child to actively participate so that he or she can learn through observation, exploration, and verbalization. Self-expression should be encouraged through writing, drawing, and movement activities.
• In an early childhood classroom, *how* the curriculum is taught is as important as *what* is taught. Process is as important as product for young children.

Overview of the Program

Children enter kindergarten if they are 5 years old by October 16. They attend the Seawell program if they live in the attendance area served by the school.

The Early Prevention of School Failure (EPSF) Program is used to assess all entering kindergarten children. The EPSF materials are designed to measure a child's relative strengths in five modalities: fine motor skills, gross motor skills, receptive and expressive language, auditory, and visual memory and visual discrimination. Children who have developmental delays in any of these areas have their classroom program individualized to meet their needs. Children with delays are retested in the spring to determine their progress.

Seawell follows the regular North Carolina school calendar. The length of the school day for elementary students is six hours. Afterschool care is available at Seawell for working parents. Children also have the opportunity to attend a variety of tuition-based afterschool enrichment activities such as math games, puppetry, breadmaking, and computer applications.

In the developmental curriculum, children develop skills in areas such as art, research, language, listening, reading, physical education, dramatic play, math, science, social studies, music, and writing. Three components of curriculum organization and three components of classroom management form the basis for the implementation of the educational program. The curriculum organization components include learning centers, skills groups, and units of study. The classroom management components include color coding, written contracts, and internal and external aspects of discipline.

Each child's progress is determined through a variety of measures. Anecdotal records, individual checklists of developmental tasks and cognitive skills, and portfolios of work are kept for each student. On a daily basis, children are given immediate feedback on products and written work. As a result, children achieve an appropriate level of mastery on one activity before beginning another. Each child also has a daily conference with the classroom teacher to review contract activities and projects. The child's work is attached to the contract and sent home each day.

Special Interdisciplinary Services

Resource teachers in art and music and the librarian meet with the children weekly. The physical education teacher is scheduled twice weekly. While the resource teachers are meeting with the children, classroom teachers are scheduled for planning periods. A "primary resource" teacher is also available to work with children who have developmental delays. Typically, a child might work with the primary resource teacher two or three times weekly for a 30-minute session.

Parent involvement is encouraged on a variety of levels. PTA functions are structured around individual classrooms rather an than entire school. For example, parents attend classroom orientations, "back-to-school" nights, and evenings where the children share their accomplishments in art, music, and physical education. Parents are encouraged to volunteer for field trips, tutoring, field days, and other classroom activities. An open visitation policy is actively encouraged by the school principal. Parents also help plan classroom enrichment activities. Newsletters and memos keep parents informed about curriculum and classroom structure.

In addition to informal contacts, parents have two regularly scheduled conferences with the classroom teacher each year. Teachers also schedule one or two night conference sessions in order to accommodate working parents. Report cards are sent to parents four times a year. In addition, standardized achievement tests are administered to the 1st graders in the spring.

Administration and Supervision of the Program

Seawell has one principal who is responsible for both curriculum and support services. Seawell is a "project school" for training student teachers for the University of North Carolina at Chapel Hill; therefore, each spring semester a supervisor of student teachers from the university works with the staff in connection with this program.

The developmental classroom is staffed by a two-teacher team and two classroom aides. Each teacher serves 26 children for a total of 52 children in the classroom setting.

Program Funding

Base funding is the same as that for all elementary programs in the state of North Carolina. The state provides $2,161 per child. This amount is supplemented locally for a total of $3,954 per child for all elementary students in the Chapel Hill system.

Program Evaluation

This program has been assessed in a variety of ways. Reading and math achievement test data were analyzed for the years 1979, 1980, 1981, and 1982. The results showed that children in this classroom scored as high as, or higher than, other children in the same school system.

During the 1986-87 school year, California Achievement Test Scores were somewhat higher in the developmental program than were the scores of other children in the same school systems (see Figure 7.2).

It has been considered equally important to analyze children's behavior and accomplishments in areas other than reading and math. Objective data concerning time on task was gathered using the Wasik-Day "Open and Traditional Learning Environments and Children's Classroom Behavior Instrument" (Day and Drake 1983). Over two years, both kindergartners and 1st graders were found to be on-task 91 percent of the time.

Special Recognition of the Program

The Seawell program is featured in ASCD's filmstrip *Early Childhood Education: Curriculum Organization and Classroom Management* and in the November 1986 issue of *Educational Leadership* in the article "Developmental and Experiential Programs: The Key to

Figure 7.2
Comparison of Achievement Scores for Seawell and District Children

	Total Reading	Language Expression	Word Analysis	Total Math
	PERCENTILE			
Seawell 1st graders	88	88	81	92
Other 1st graders	72	72	62	82

Quality Education and Care of Young Children." Further information about how to implement the developmental classroom can be found in the text that accompanies the filmstrip (Day and Drake 1983).

Program Strengths

The strength of this program has been its ability to translate developmental theory into clearly articulated educational practice. The program features a wide range of materials and activities that are appropriate for young children. Imagination, creativity, verbal expression, and psychomotor activities are incorporated into the curriculum, along with a traditional emphasis on the sciences and cognitive skills. A wide variety of skill levels are also addressed within each area of emphasis. The program features an effective management system that is clear to both teachers and children. The management system, based on contracts and color-coding, is essential to the success of this multi-task setting. In addition, high expectations for students and careful monitoring of student progress are an integral part of the learning environment.

References

Bloom, B.S. *All the Children Learning*. New York: McGraw Hill, 1981.
Carroll, J.B. "A Model of School Learning." *Teachers College Record* 64 (1963): 723-733.
Day, B.D., and K.N. Drake. *Early Childhood Education: Curriculum Organization and Classroom Management*. Alexandria, Va.: Association for Supervision and Curriculum Development, 1983.
Day, B.D., and K.N. Drake. "Developmental and Experiential Programs: The Key to Quality Education and Care of Young Children." *Educational Leadership* 44 (November 1986): 24-27.
Elkind, D. "Formal Education and Early Childhood Education: An Essential Difference." *Phi Delta Kappan* 67 (1986): 631-636.
Piaget, J. *The Origins of Intelligence in Children*. New York: International Universities Press, 1952.

Statewide Programs for 4-Year-Olds: The South Carolina Model

Contact: Janet Perry, Early Childhood Education Consultant
South Carolina Half-Day Child Development Program for
4-Year-Olds
State Department of Education
808 Rutledge Building
Columbia, SC 29201
(803) 734-8355

Background of the Program

In 1984, the South Carolina legislature passed the Education Improvement Act of 1984 (EIA) providing funds to the State Department of Education to serve a target population of 4-year-olds who had been identified as having "predicted readiness deficiencies." During the fifth year of implementation (1988-89), 10,700 children will be served. These are children who have been deemed by local districts as being at risk for school failure.

To determine eligibility, districts must incorporate the DIAL-R (Mardell-Czudnowski and Goldenberg 1983) and weigh additional predictable at-risk criteria such as family income or the educational level of the mother. After all criteria is weighed, children can be ranked from "most-at-risk" to "least-at-risk." Children deemed "not-at-risk" are not eligible. Enrollment criteria also include standards that address children with developmental delays who cannot effectively be served in the program.

Program Mission

The goal of the program is to reduce the number of children unable to achieve success in school. It will provide a developmental educational program for 10,700 4-year-olds by the end of a 5-year phase-in period in 1988-89.

Program Overview

The High/Scope Preschool Curriculum, developed by the High/Scope Foundation (Hohmann et al. 1978), was selected for staff training because it was philosophically compatible with the statewide kindergarten program and because media and training resources were available to meet the regulatory requirement for staff development.

The program model has two components. A classroom component is characterized by child- and teacher-initiated activities in children's interest centers. The outreach component, used on a limited basis, is a program of home visits for hard-to-reach parents and children.

Continuous assessment of child progress is mandatory, but no specific document is required for use statewide. The extent to which health services, social services, and other educational services (such as speech therapy) are provided depends on district resources and child needs. Services for children identified as handicapped are provided based on the child's individualized educational plan (IEP).

Programs operate at least 180 days per school year, with at least 2½ hours of instructional time per day (excluding breakfast, lunch, and transportation). Each classroom is staffed by a teacher certified in early childhood and an aide. Each teacher and aide team serves 2 groups of 20 children each day.

Two parent conferences and two home visits are required within the 180-day period. Other parent activities such as school visits and parent meetings are strongly encouraged.

Child development programs are administered and supervised by the school principals in local school districts. District contact persons are assigned to coordinate local funding, regulations, and classroom activities with state program requirements. State early childhood education consultants monitor regulatory requirements and provide technical assistance for program implementation to all districts annually.

Program Evaluation

The efficacy of the EIA child development programs was judged to have a positive effect on school readiness as evaluated in part by the State Department of Education and in part under contract by researchers at Utah State University. Two complementary research designs were employed: a statewide study using data on all children who entered 1st grade in 1986 and a more targeted research sample from three regions, which studied test scores at kindergarten entry, adding data on program quality and eliminating self-selection bias.

The findings of a study completed in the fall of 1986 also point to program effectiveness. The final results of the statewide study will be completed in the spring of 1990.

Program Funding

The child development program is funded entirely with state monies. A summary of enrollment and funding is below, including the 1983-84 pilot year.

Year	Funds	Children Served
1983-84	918,918	1,050
1984-85	1,860,067	3,365
1985-86	6,281,432	6,715
1986-87	6,866,613	7,943
1987-88	8,255,924	8,451

Strongest Element of the Program

The strongest element of the program is the state's extensive commitment to improving students' school success by addressing their education at an early age. Through state interagency planning and support, the statewide early childhood program was funded for a specific target population. As a result, children who have had few early learning experiences have the opportunity to attend a program specifically designed to meet their needs and build a base for continued school success.

References

Hohmann, Mary, B. Banet, and D. Weikart. *Young Children in Action.* Ypsilanti, Mich.: The High/Scope Press, 1978.

Mardell-Czudnowski, Carol D., and Dorethea S. Goldenberg. *DIAL-R— Developmental Indicators for the Assessment of Learning, Rev.* Edison, N.J.: Childcraft Education Corp., 1983.

Exploring Excellence for Young Children: Pasco, Washington

Contact: Stephanie Tesch
Assistant Superintendent
Pasco School District #1
1004 N. 16th Ave.
Pasco, WA 99301
(509) 547-9531

Background of the Program

The program is located in Pasco, Washington, which has a total of approximately 6,000 students, 800 of whom are enrolled in early childhood programs. The early childhood effort affects all eight elementary schools and encompasses at-risk preschool children (characteristics include low income, limited English proficient [5 languages], migrant, remedial, special needs learners), all kindergartners, and a transition population between kindergarten and 1st grade.

The program began with a year of planning and needs assessment and developed into a major effort the following year. That effort began with an attempt to improve learning for children ages 4-7 and an attempt to better organize and coordinate educational opportunities for small children. The initial development began in a cooperative fashion between the district language committee and support services personnel, growing to encompass the entire district.

Program Mission

The major goal of the program is to prevent school failure in later years. The program is based on the belief that if children are successful in school by the age 6 or 7, they will be much more likely to be successful throughout their school experience. Especially at risk in our population are other-language children (30 percent). Efforts are especially, but not exclusively, focused on this population.

Overview of the Program

In the preschool programs, high-risk children are either limited English proficient, low income, or qualify for special education support. All-day/everyday kindergarten programs serve 60 percent high-risk children and 40 percent children who have no special learning needs. Extended day kindergarten serves only high-risk children.

Both preschool and kindergarten are scheduled for a half day for most children. Three district classrooms are all-day/everyday. Currently, one school is piloting an extended day kindergarten program. The transition program, scheduled for all day, serves approximately 50 children who need additional assistance in adjusting to 1st grade.

All curriculums for Pasco's young children have a language development emphasis. Concept learning in each curricular area is tied closely to language development. Children are involved in their own learning, and many of the activities are experiential.

The district has developed student learning objectives for children aged 4-7 across all curricular areas. Examples of curriculum used in this fashion are "Math Their Way" and the use of the whole language approach in the instruction of language arts and reading readiness. "Math Their Way" is a hands-on program that is highly involved with manipulatives and language interaction. Whole language develops language and reading readiness with much teacher-child interaction that is based on children's literature, a child's own language, and a child's own writing based on his or her language.

The district uses small group instruction with instructional aides wherever possible. These small groups are a part of standard classrooms of approximately 25 children.

There is minimal parent involvement, but regular conferences and building visits take place in each school.

Administration and Supervision

Supervision is by the building principal. Preschool, all-day/everyday kindergarten, the extended day pilot, and the transition program each have a certified teacher and classroom aides. The standard half-day kindergarten program has minimal aide support.

Program Evaluation

The district has produced extensive evidence from the bilingual program that the efforts are successful for the children. Evaluation of the early childhood education program for five groups of children has been done from 1982-83 through 1986-87. There have been follow-up studies at the kindergarten level for the first four years and at the end of 1st grade for the first two years. Children made gains in reading, math, handwriting, and English vocabulary. The complete study is available from Beverly McConnell, Southwest 614 Cityview, Pullman, WA 99163 for $10.

Program Funding

The program development is funded largely through district monies. Support for classroom teachers with high-risk children is available through bilingual, Migrant, Chapter I, and Special Education funds. Chapter II has provided some evaluation and committee work. Since this is a comprehensive program for ages 4-7, it is not program driven. The process is district supported, and monies from categorical funds are plugged in where appropriate and when available.

Major Strength of Program

The program has longevity in the district. Beginning in the mid-1970s, efforts were undertaken to provide school district program developers with solid information about programs for young children. Subsequently, efforts were not targeted at just one group or at one area of the curriculum.

State and Nationally Accredited Prekindergarten Program: Baltimore City Public Schools

Contact: Carla Brewington-Ford, Supervisor
Baltimore City Public Schools
200 East North Ave.
Baltimore, MD 21202

Background of the Program

Established during the 1960s with funds granted by the Ford Foundation, preschool programs in the Baltimore City Public Schools (BCPS) were designed to prevent educational failure in future years. All programs incorporated three major elements: instructional support services, a continuum of instructional experiences, and parent involvement and education.

Today, approximately 3,600 4-year-old students attend prekindergarten in the Baltimore City Public Schools. These programs are now located in 86 elementary schools in the district. While the majority of schools with prekindergarten programs are located in historically economically and educationally underprivileged areas, several schools provide these programs to students with middle class backgrounds. A large number of at-risk students are served, including Chapter I and State Compensatory Education eligible pupils. Intellectual ranges vary.

To be eligible for the program, students must:
• live within the school zone
• be 4 years old by December 31
• receive all required immunizations

Students in Chapter I and State Compensatory Education Programs must meet federal criteria for family educational economic deprivation.

Program Mission

The overall goal of the program is to provide experiences that promote the cognitive, emotional, social, and physical development of young children. Subgoals are:
• To enhance and reinforce the development of expressive and receptive language in all areas of the curriculum.
• To enhance the development of gross and fine motor skills.

• To enhance positive self-concept, self-reliance, and motivations for learning.

• To foster creativity and expansion of ideas through a variety of media.

• To provide active learning experiences that develop competencies in acquiring concepts and enhance thinking.

• To ensure a safe and developmentally appropriate environment.

Overview of the Program

Emphasis is placed on consideration of the strengths, interests, needs, and diverse backgrounds that young children bring to school. Teachers are required to plan activities that allow for active exploration and utilization of all sensory areas and use of developmentally appropriate materials and settings. Teachers use the "Basic Learnings Objectives" guide (Brewington-Ford et al. 1987) in planning educational activities. The guide provides direction for daily and long-range planning, monitoring student progress, and planning parent involvement activities. Teachers rely on an integrated, thematic unit approach, defined here as an instructional plan incorporating basic concepts from many subject areas. The approach includes small- and large-group activities. Concrete objects, manipulatives, and instructional equipment are available, and children have the freedom to select instructional activities and materials. Learning centers are used to reinforce, apply and extend skills. Classes meet for 2½ hours daily.

Each class is assigned an early childhood certified teacher and an aide. The teacher/pupil ratio is 1:10. Class size is limited to no more than 20 students. Currently, 102 teachers and aides are assigned to the program.

Parents are important contributors to the total educational program. Parents help plan the educational program for their children, help carry it out, and help evaluate its success. Many schools have a school-community liaison worker who recruits parents to serve in parent councils and in the classrooms as volunteers. Principals and teachers encourage parents to participate in training sessions so they can better understand the characteristics of children and how the prekindergarten program supports their child's growth. Parent discussion groups with community leaders and outside agency representatives are regularly scheduled as a means to improve parent effectiveness.

Administration and Supervision of the Program

The program is administered in collaboration with the local school principal, district Executive Director, and the Supervisor of the Office of Early Childhood Education. Additionally, early childhood educational specialists and master teachers provide biweekly technical assistance, staff development, and direct supervision to all teachers and aides. Two prekindergarten program facilitators monitor the program and provide training to all staff members involved.

Program Evaluation

Year-to-Year Comparison. Prekindergarten pupils are tested each fall and spring using the Boehm Test of Basic Concepts (Boehm 1986). The test addresses whether the pupil understands concepts such as space, quantity, and time. Children's fall and spring raw scores, total scores, and percentage correct for each item are analyzed.

Longitudinal Studies. In 1986, the Office of Testing and Evaluation completed phase one of a seven-year longitudinal study of children with and without experience in the BCSP prekindergarten program. Two longitudinal groups of pupils entering BCPS were established for FY 83 and FY 84. These pupils were then at grades 2 and 1, respectively. Preliminary findings support the following:

• Pupils exposed to early childhood experiences in BCPS outperformed pupils who enter BCPS at grade 1.

• Children not exposed to the BCPS early childhood programs tend to have lower than average reading, vocabulary, and math skills.

Of particular interest was the finding that movement from school to school may expose pupils to a disruptive educational experience. Children who move tend to exhibit lower scores.

Overall, the initial longitudinal sample indicates positive outcomes. Phase II of the study will follow the students through the 7th grade.

Special Recognition/Acknowledgment for the Program

In 1985, the National Academy of Early Childhood Program— the department of the National Association for the Education of Young Children (NAEYC) that administers accreditation to early childhood programs that function in accordance with the criteria for high quality programs—completed its review of the prekindergarten center in Tench Tilghman Elementary School, Baltimore City Public Schools. Following a self-study of the center's operations, a written report to Academy by school staff concerning the self-study results, and a visit by early childhood validators, the center became the first public school preschool program in the nation to receive accreditation. George G. Kelson Elementary Schools, Baltimore city, was also accredited by the Academy.

Program Funding

The program is budgeted for over $4.7 million. The federal government provides $3.5 million through Chapter I and approximately $200,000 through SEC. The state department of education provides almost $1.1 million.

Unique Design Feature of the Program

The unique feature of this program is the "Basic Learnings Objectives" guide that enables teachers to provide for learning development based on an appropriate sequence of learning within and across curriculum strands. Teachers are able to identify entry-level behaviors and to plan an instructional program geared to meet the needs of individual students.

References

Boehm, A. *Boehm Test of Basic Concepts, revised*. Psychology Corporation, 1986.
Brewington-Ford, C., P. Glassman, L. Schwartzman, C. Weidel, and D. Wortham. "Basic Learnings Objectives" guide. Baltimore: Office of Early Childhood Education, Baltimore City Public Schools, 1987.

Academic Kindergarten:
School District of Philadelphia

Contact: Leontine D. Scott
Associate Superintendent for School Operations
Room 601 Administration Bldg.
School District of Philadelphia
21st and The Parkway
Philadelphia, PA 19103
(215) 299-7665

Background of the Program

Systemwide kindergartens were established in Philadelphia in the mid-1870s. Although there are state subsidies, kindergarten is still not state mandated. The program operates at least a half day every weekday throughout the school year, with at least 169 full-day kindergartens in operation as of 1987-88.

Program Mission

The major goal of the program is to meet the educational/developmental, physical, emotional, and social needs of 4.7 to 5.7 year olds (approximately 15,000 students).

Overview of the Program

Children are admitted into the program on a first-come, first-served basis. They receive health screening only.

The curriculum follows the district's kindergarten curriculum. There is a standardized kindergarten curriculum that is a downward extension of the school district's new standardized curriculum for grades 1-12. The standardized curriculum is a translation of the system's goals and objectives into a functional instructional program and the means of simultaneously promoting excellence and equity. The content and skills appropriate for kindergartners are clearly outlined in terms of scope and sequence. While Philadelphia's kindergartens are academically oriented in the sense of being responsible for implementing the standardized curriculum, they give equal emphasis to the principles of child development in satisfying this responsibility, and they place the highest value on each child's attainment of developmental maturity. Kindergarten teachers, moreover, are not obliged to use any specific instructional approach but are free to exhibit their competence in a variety of ways ranging from highly structured direct instruction strategies to methods that feature child-initiated activities facilitated by expert adults.

Parent volunteers are recruited to assist in the classroom. Each school has a Home and School Association.

The program is administered by one associate superintendent and four supervisors. There are approximately 350 teachers and 175 paraprofessionals districtwide.

Program Evaluation

Students in the program have consistently performed well, especially in mathematics, on citywide tests.

Program Funding

The program receives substantial state subsidies but is funded in large part through the district's operating budget. The operating cost is approximately $1,000 per child.

Unique Element of the Program

The program has provided a consistently sound academic/developmental experience and introduction to schooling for the majority of students in the school district for more than 100 years.

The district also serves young children through several other districtwide programs. The district child care program, serving 1,400 children aged 3 months to 11, provides year-round care on a daily basis. The district's day-care component, funded by Title XX funds, operates 44 centers that provide 24-hour care to approximately 2,400 children 2 to 11. Established in the mid-1950s, the district's parent cooperative nurseries provide active involvement of approximately 400 4-year-old children and their parents in a developmental preschool setting. Finally, the district's prekindergarten Head Start Program operates 29 centers for 3- and 4-year-old children from poverty-level families.

Head Start-Preschool Handicapped Program: Johnson County Schools

Contact: Ann M. Hampton, Director
211 N. Church St.
Mountain City, TN 37683
(615) 727-7911

Background of the Program

As a delegate agency, Johnson County Schools began operating Head Start in the summer of 1965. In 1971, Head Start became a year-round program in the district, and in 1978 a preschool program for handicapped children was added to operate cooperatively with the Head Start and kindergarten programs. For the past four years, services have been provided in Mountain City Elementary, a school for preschool-6th grade.

Head Start currently serves 40 children, and the preschool handicapped program serves approximately 20 children. Ages of children range from 3 to 5 years. Most 5-year-olds, however, meet developmental criteria and are served in the district's kindergarten program.

Children served by Head Start often enter school with health problems and a lack of self-confidence. Local medical providers and the Tennessee Child Health and Development Program refer children in need of an environment that will meet their total developmental needs, especially the need for socialization. Other children served in this program are those who show developmental delay in more than one area assessed during the annual systemwide screening program.

Program Mission

Head Start was designed to provide preschool children of low-income families with a comprehensive program to meet their emotional, social, health, nutritional, and psychological needs. There are four major components of Head Start: education, health, parent involvement, and social services. The major goal of the Johnson County Preschool Program is to assure to the greatest extent possible the early identification of young children's developmental needs and to work together with parents to achieve effective intervention.

Overview of the Program

Every child receives a variety of learning experiences, both in the classroom and through home visits, to foster intellectual, social, and emotional growth. Children are encouraged to express their feelings and to develop self-confidence and the ability to get along with others.

Each child is assessed using Griffin and Sanford's *Learning Accomplishment Profile-Diagnostic* (LAP-D). This assessment is designed to provide teachers of young children (in particular those with special needs) with a criterion-referenced record of the child's existing skills. Use of the LAP-D enables the teacher to identify developmentally appropriate learning objectives for each child, measure progress through changes in rate of development, and provide specific information relevant to pupil learning.

Curriculum units and learning activities address a child's needs found through assessment of the child's existing skills. The curriculum focuses on six areas of development: gross motor, fine motor, social, self help, cognitive, and language. The curriculum is based upon *A Planning Guide: The Preschool Curriculum* prepared by Chapel Hill Training-Outreach Program (Findlay et al. 1983). This book contains topical units arranged in a sequence of daily activities. Included are correlated curriculum materials and multisensory activities that provide for individual differences in children. The curriculum stresses language arts (listening, speaking, and prereading skill) through the use of books, stories or poetry, fingerplays, and dramatization. Science is integrated into the curriculum through observation of plants and animals, discussion of seasons of the year, sand and water play, and food preparation activities. Mathematics is taught directly and indirectly through introduction of number concepts and plane geometry (identification of circles, triangles, squares, and rectangles). The curriculum also includes daily experiences in art, music, movement education, health, nutrition, and social studies (effective experiences to promote development of communication skills, respectful human relationships, and appropriate social behavior). Activities progress from simple to complex, from concrete to abstract, and result from spontaneous child-initiated and teacher-initiated experiences.

The teaching procedures reflect strategies of task analysis, reverse chaining, and positive reinforcement. Learning activities provided in the classroom are also incorporated into a home follow-up program.

For the homebound child with severe handicaps, home counseling and educational sessions are provided regularly. Preschool/ Head Start staff members work with the school psychologist in developing and implementing weekly sessions for one-on-one behavior tutoring for children who have demonstrated a need for increased appropriate behaviors in order to participate in a group setting. Johnson County Schools also work closely with other programs that provide services to at-risk and handicapped children.

Operational Details of the Program

Eligibility for Head Start is based on family size and income, with preference given to children from families with the most need. Children enrolled must be between the age of 3 and compulsory school age. Johnson County serves primarily 4-year-olds. Three- and 4-year-old children who appear to be delayed or who have been determined to need special services, and who do not meet economic criteria for Head Start, are enrolled in the district preschool handicap program.

Three- and 4-year-olds have the option of attending two or four days per week, depending on their needs. They receive either monthly or biweekly home visits. Children attend school for 6½ hours each day unless there is a need to modify the length.

Since the program is founded on the premise that parents are the most important influence on a child's development, their involvement in the classroom and during home visits is essential. Parents are encouraged to participate in their child's program both at home and as volunteers in the classroom. They assist in program planning and evaluation. Some of the parents serve on Policy Committees where they have a voice in administrative and managerial decisions.

Administration and Supervision of the Program

The Upper East Tennessee Human Development Agency (UETHDA) is the grantee for the Head Start Program. Johnson County Schools serves as a delegate agency that operates the program in Johnson County. The Head Start program follows policies and guidelines of both the Johnson County Board of Education and the UETHDA Board of Directors. A part-time director administers the Head Start Program and coordinates educational and special services for both the preschool and Head Start Programs.

Head Start has two full-time teachers who meet Tennessee certification requirements for serving young children. Two paraprofessionals serve as teacher assistants and family service workers. A special services aide assists in the classroom with children who have severe disabilities. Preschool handicapped staff and school system support staff provide speech, language and academic resource and consulting services. Related services such as occupational and physical therapy or vision and hearing technical assistance, are provided by the school system through contractual agreements.

Program Evaluation

A study that evaluated the impact of Head Start on the cognitive development of children indicated that the children tended to score higher than comparable non-Head Start children on preschool achievement tests that measure cognitive abilities (McKey et al. 1985). This study also showed that Head Start children performed equal to or better than their peers when they entered regular school, and there were fewer grade retentions and special class placements.

Local program evaluation addresses both child growth and overall program impact. Criterion-referenced testing, parent interviews, and observational data indicate surprising gains for many of the children. Data obtained from questionnaires and interviews indicate that parents value the preschool/Head Start experience for their children and recognize potential benefits to the children as well as to themselves.

Program Funding

The federal government funds $75,598 for Head Start. Approximately $30,186 comes from nonfederal sources. The Preschool Incentive Program receives $7,242 from the state (EHA, Part B—Federal Funds).

Strongest Feature of the Program

Head Start in Johnson County is an integral part of the local education system. The program uses school resources, conducts joint staff training, and develops cooperative policy statements. Over the years, Head Start program concepts and practices have been transferred to the regular school program, including such practices as use of paraprofessionals, increased parent involvement, adoption of culturally responsive curriculums, establishment of programs for younger children, and comprehensive services to meet entire family needs. The collaborative effort between the Preschool Handicap Program and Head Start has offered children with special needs a full range of developmental services in a group with other children rather than in a separate group for the handicapped.

References

Findlay, J., P. Miller, A. Pegram, L. Richey, A. Sanford, and B. Semrau. *A Planning Guide: The Preschool Curriculum*. Prepared by Chapel Hill Training-Outreach Program. Winston Salem, N.C.: Kaplan Press, 1983.

LeMay, D.W., P.M. Griffin, and A.R. Sanford, "Learning Accomplishment Profile-Diagnostic (LAP-D). Chapel Hill Training-Outreach Program.

McKey, R.H., L. Condelli, H. Ganson, B. Barrett, C. McConkey, and M.C. Plantz. *The Impact of Head Start on Children, Families and Communities*. Final Report of the Head Start Evaluation, Synthesis and Utilization Project. June 1985. Contract No. 105-81-C-026.

New York State Prekindergarten Program: New York City Public Schools

Contact: Marjorie McAllister, Director
Early Childhood Education Unit
131 Livingston St.
Brooklyn, NY 11201
(718) 935-4255

Background of the Program

The New York State Prekindergarten Program started in New York City in 1966 with 65 classrooms in 24 elementary schools. During the 1986-87 school year, more that 2,800 children participated in the program in 72 schools in 21 community school districts.

Program Mission

The goals of the program are:
- To foster a sense of trust in a public school environment.
- To develop feelings of confidence and self-worth.
- To encourage the integration of communication arts.
- To enhance thinking skills and decision making.
- To develop problem solving capabilities.
- To develop self-discipline.

The program gives special attention to the individual learning style of each child, taking into account differences in rates and modes of learning. Self-initiated and independent activities are reinforced as teachers observe, interact with children, and provide a rich learning environment. Continuity is encouraged as the children move through the early childhood grades.

Overview of the Program

The curriculum, as described in the teacher handbook *Three, Four, Open The Door* (New York City Board of Education 1986), uses the child's interests and experiences to develop the appropriate skills. The instructional approach is activity/child centered. The experiences for children are based on their interests, needs, and strengths. Facilities, equipment, materials, and activities are chosen to capitalize on the ways children learn. The teacher and educational assistant guide the learning through firsthand experience. The staff facilitates curriculum development by enabling children to discover and understand.

Eligibility for the program is based on New York State Education Department guidelines. At least 90 percent of the children selected must be from economically disadvantaged families.

Guidelines specify a complete health screening and immunization for each child. No other screening or testing is required.

New York state prekindergarten is a 2½-hour program with separate morning and afternoon groups. Children are served a family style lunch in the classroom. Daily outdoor activity is planned.

The prekindergarten program reinforces the importance of home and emphasizes the contribution of the parent as the first teacher. Parents are involved in a number of ways, including:

- Participation in the school and classroom activities.
- Interaction with staff during home/school visits.
- Attendance at workshops on child-rearing practices/skills.
- Service on decision-making committees.

A family room in each school is the center for parent involvement activities.

Administration and Supervision of the Program

The program is approved and monitored by the Bureau of Child Development and Parent Education of the New York State Education Department. The director and the assistant director of the Early Childhood Education Unit are responsible for supervising and providing technical assistance to the district early childhood coordinator/director, who is chiefly responsible for the implementation of the program.

A licensed teacher and educational assistant (paraprofessional) are assigned to each prekindergarten classroom. A licensed social worker and/or family assistant (paraprofessional) provide social services.

Program Evaluation

The State Education Department conducted a longitudinal evaluation of the New York State Prekindergarten Program. Findings in the study indicate that:

- Children who attend the prekindergarten classes have an advantage over similar children when they enter kindergarten in their mastery of knowledge and skills judged to be important in coping with school tasks.
- Prekindergarten has a favorable impact across grades on children's knowledge of verbal concepts.

• Children with more exposure to prekindergarten tend to receive higher ratings on social competency.

• Children with more exposure to prekindergarten tend to be rated higher on task orientation by their teachers at the end of the program.

• When parents become involved in the program, their children score better on measures of cognitive performance.

• Children from the prekindergarten programs are more likely to make normal progress through the primary grades.

• Fewer former prekindergarten children than control-group children repeat grades or are placed in special education classes.

Program Funding

Funding for the 1986-87 school year was:

7,707,410	State Education Department	89%
952,613	Local District Funds	11%
8,660,023	**Total**	

These funds provided programs for 2,870 prekindergarten children.

It should be noted that there were 7,216 preschool children in New York City for the 1987-88 school year. Of these, 2,870 were funded by the New York State Prekindergarten Program. Other funding sources included New York State Legislative grants, Chapter I, Project Giant Step, and local district funds.

Strongest Element of the Program

The strongest element in the program is involvement of parents. The literature and research in early childhood education is filled with recommendations about the importance of involving parents in support of child learning and development. Therefore, each school has a family room that is a center for parent meetings and workshops—for parent learning and growth—that strengthen the home/school connection.

Reference

New York City Board of Education. *Three, Four, Open the Door.* New York: Board of Education of the City of New York, 1986.

Cognitively Oriented Preschool Curriculum: Fairfax County Head Start Program

Contact: Sandy Lowe
Fairfax Department of Community Action
Fair Oaks Corporate Center
11216 Waples Mill Rd.
Fairfax, VA 22030
(703) 246-5171

Background of the Program

Since the early 1960s, the Head Start program and the High/Scope Educational Research Foundation in Ypsilanti, Michigan, have been inextricably bound together. Fairfax County uses as its primary curriculum guide for its Head Start program *Young Children in Action, a Manual for Preschool Educators* (Hohmann et al. 1979).

In Fairfax County, approximately 1,100 low-income preschool children participate in Head Start. In the 1987-88 school year, 1,100 Head Start students from approximately 820 families were served through 106 classrooms and home-based models in 86 sites throughout the county. The program serves primarily 3- and 4-year-olds, representing a wide range of developmental and intellectual capacities, in preparation for attending kindergarten in the public schools. Specific enrollment priorities include special needs children, children referred by protective services agencies, children in single-parent female-headed households, and children in families receiving Aid to Families with Dependent Children. Approximately 18 percent of all Head Start children served in fiscal year 1986 were handicapped. There are 26 languages and cultures represented in Fairfax County Head Start classrooms.

Program Mission

Head Start services include education, social and health services and parent involvement.

The mission of the program is to meet the diverse needs of children and their families, to foster improved health status, to stimulate gains in cognitive and language skills development, to encourage intellectual curiosity, to develop self-confidence and self-sufficiency, and to strengthen the involvement of parents in their children's education. To fulfill this mission, the Fairfax County Head Start program has implemented a number of innovative and substantive approaches to service delivery. Performing arts exposure through collaboration with the Wolf Trap Performing Arts Foundation, computer assisted instruction, multicultural mini-classrooms, and the 6th grader placement program are a few examples of these approaches. The implementation of the Cognitively Oriented Preschool Curriculum is one more step in providing enhanced academic and administrative support to the program.

Overview of the Program

The Fairfax County Head Start Program provides a developmental program that offers individualized learning experiences geared to each child's level of cognitive development, the goal being to stimulate progress toward the highest level of achievement and ability. The curriculum offers specific methods for addressing the following priorities of the program:
- provision of a clear and consistent instructional philosophy
- organized content/skill objectives and strategies
- classroom arrangement and management procedures
- ongoing student assessment methodologies
- systematic teacher training and evaluation methods

The content of the curriculum consists of 50 key experiences organized within 8 categories: active learning, language experiencing, language representing, classification, seriation, numbers, spatial relations, and time.

The Cognitively Oriented Preschool Curriculum is based on Piaget's constructs of child development and focuses on the preoperational stage. Active learning, where the learner initiates direct interaction with people, objects, and events, is the process used in the cognitively oriented curriculum. In the process of active learning, the learner is engaged in constructing a theory of reality by initiating sensorimotor actions, which lead to mental operations. The key experiences in active learning are:
- Exploring actively with all senses.
- Discovering relations through direct experience.
- Manipulating, transforming and combining materials.
- Choosing materials, activities, purposes.
- Acquiring skills with tools and equipment.
- Using the large muscles.
- Taking care of one's own needs (Hohmann et al. 1979).

The educational philosophy of the program is reflected in the way the classroom is arranged. In the cognitively oriented classroom space, furniture and materials are arranged to define logically organized and labeled work areas and to give children the opportunity to make choices and to have control over the classroom environment. A consistent daily routine helps the preschooler understand time and enables both teacher and child to plan for the day.

Operational Details of the Program

The curriculum is not dependent on any particular testing or screening methodology. Currently, the Head Start program in Fairfax County uses the Denver Developmental Srceening Test for testing purposes.

Parent involvement is a basic tenet of the Head Start program and of this curriculum. A subsection of the curriculum describes ways that parents can be used as classroom resources.

The program is administered by the Department of Community Action (DCA). Services are provided by three delegate agencies: the Fairfax County Public Schools and two community based organizations, Higher Horizons and Saunders B. Moon. The Head Start Coordinator, employed by DCA, is responsible for overall grant administration, coordination of delegate agency activities, linkage with other DCA resources and program services, and annual Head Start training.

The initial step in implementing the curriculum was to have staff trained as trainers by the High/Scope Educational Research Foundation. This was accomplished in 1984-85 when 11 area teachers participated in a "Trainer of Trainers" project. From that initial group, an individual was selected to be the first trainer on the Fairfax County Head Start staff. Each year since, a group of Head Start teachers has received training in the use of the curriculum. In the 1985-86 school year, 12 teachers and 5 aides were trained in the use of the curriculum. In the 1986-87 school year, 17 teachers and 13 aides were trained. It is the intent of the program to have trained all classroom staff in the use of the curriculum by 1990. One High/Scope trainer is responsible for all training activities and reports directly to the executive director.

Program Evaluation

The curriculum and its use have been continually assessed by the High/Scope Foundation since it began over 20 years ago. In the summer of 1987, the Fairfax County Head Start program initiated a major study of Head Start participants. This longitudinal study includes data on Head Start children for each school year from 1982-83 through 1988-89. One dimension of the study compares the performance of children who participated in the Cognitively Oriented Preschool Curriculum with the performance of those who did not.

Recognition of the Program

In 1986-87, the program received accreditation for undergraduate credit from Northern Virginia Community College and for graduate credit from the University of the District of Columbia.

Fairfax County has been officially recognized on the High/Scope Educational Research Foundation registry as a training center for Region III. A training center offers training of trainers, training of teachers, and training for administrators on a tuition basis to area Head Start agencies. The center also provides training for Fairfax County staff members.

Program Funding

Head Start funds training and tuition payments by other local jurisdictions that choose to use our services.

The costs for implementing this curriculum, which may be significantly different from other curriculums, are the cost of training and supporting a certified trainer, the cost of release time for teaching staff to attend training (approximately 8 weeks) and the cost of the curriculum materials (approximately $100 per trainee).

Program Strengths

The cognitively Oriented Preschool Curriculum has provided many benefits to the Fairfax County Head Start program and has many strengths at various levels of the program. For the Head Start child and teacher it provides a physical environment and methods for systematic adult-child interactions that conform with the child's developmental needs. For the teaching staff, it provides methods for planning and working as a supportive team. For parents and teachers, it addresses parents' roles as educators of their children and resources for the classroom. For teachers and supervisors, it provides an ongoing program of training and supervision. It provides administrators a systematic process of staff development and program assessment.

Reference

Hohmann, Mary, Bernard Banet, and David P. Weikart. *Young Children in Action: A Manual for Preschool Educators.* Ypsilanti, Mich.: High/Scope Press, 1979.

A Joint Venture Between Two Districts: Affton-Lindbergh Early Childhood Education Program

Contact: Elma Armistead, Associate Superintendent
Sheila Sherman, Director of Early Childhood and
    Principal
Lindbergh School District
1225 Eddie and Park
Sunset Hills, MO 63127

Background of Program

The Affton-Lindbergh Early Childhood Education Program originated in Affton School District in 1970. Because declining enrollment had resulted in empty classrooms, a kindergarten teacher and two aides were assigned to set up a preschool program. Many children were enrolled for both morning and afternoon sessions—a clear indication that working parents were seeking a safe, secure environment for their children. When those same students entered kindergarten a few years later, their parents expressed an interest in extended care. Affton responded by creating a kindergarten extended day program. The district also established a care service both before and after elementary classes. In 1982, a parent-toddler program was created to provide families with support, information, and a fun place to make new friends.

The program continued to develop and respond to community needs. By 1984, it served over 2,000 families and required additional space.

The Lindbergh School Board, which had space to offer and an interest in providing enrichment to the children in the district, agreed to house the program in its Harry S. Truman School.

The Affton-Lindbergh Early Childhood Program, under the sponsorship of two school districts, is a self-sustaining program for children ages 6 weeks to 11 years. It offers many services, including special education, individual diagnostic services, and day care.

Program Mission

The goal of the program is to constantly and consistently help families make a positive contribution to their child's first venture into education and the community. Through this early educational experience, children form a foundation for independence, success, productivity, and contentment.

Overview of the Program

The Affton-Lindbergh Early Childhood Education Program is made up of 8 different programs, accommodating 940 children. The staff consists of 72 teachers, 1 director, and 1 assistant director.

Early Childhood Education. Serves children 2½ to 5 years of age. Available for three hours, morning or afternoon. The program is based on the High/Scope Cognitively Oriented Curriculum (Hohmann 1979), which promotes independence and enhances thinking skills.

Early Childhood Extended Day. Offers families year-round care from 6:30 A.M. to 6:00 P.M. Activities are also built around the High/Scope Cognitively Oriented Curriculum, an approach to preschool education that stresses hands-on activities for appropriate work and play.

Kindergarten Extended Day. Children may attend either morning or afternoon classes at their regular school to be eligible for this program. The curriculum is organized around art, science, language experiences, music, physical development, and dramatic activities. All-day care is available on most major holidays and when school is not in session due to bad weather or teacher conferences.

Developmental Kindergarten. An after-school enrichment program for children with special needs. Children are admitted based on results of the Missouri KIDS test or recommendation of a classroom teacher.

School Age Extended Day. Students in grades 1 through 6 can enroll in before school and afterschool sessions. Before school, children are transported by parents to the program. After school, students arrive by bus from other elementary schools in the communities. This program is in session during holidays, summer recess and on snow days.

Parents as First Teachers. An early learning program for both parents and young children, Parents as First Teachers is designed to reduce the stress of nurturing active children. Parents receive information about skills and development appropriate to every stage of the child's early years.

Parent-Toddler Education. For children aged 18-36 months, parent-toddler classes meet for two hours, once a week, for 12 weeks. Parents and toddlers are together for the first hour of each session; they are separated during the last hour so that parents can discuss their children.

Special Education. Free developmental screening is offered to any child 5 years of age or younger, with approximately a third of the children (or 150) showing a need for special help. An individualized educational plan (IEP) is designed for each child to help strengthen skills needed for successful school experience.

All learning experiences in the early childhood programs are based on the High/Scope Cognitively Oriented Curriculum, which focuses on two major questions: How does a child think, and how can we support this thinking? The curriculum includes eight key experiences: seriation, classification, representation, number, time, space, active learning, and language. The thrust is for children to actively construct their learning by using their senses; using tools effectively (tools being defined as everything from pencils to mixing spoons, to blocks); by speaking and listening; incorporating the whole language approach; and by representing—drawing, painting, relating photos to real objects, role playing, and imitation.

The curriculum is child-initiated with the core of the program being to "Plan, Do, and Review." Children make choices about how to spend their time. The teacher observes, using the information gained to provide opportunities for developmentally appropriate experiences.

Staff members record the child's daily progress in relation to the key experiences. A developmental checklist assists the evaluation of age-appropriate tasks. Children are screened via the DENVER developmental screening test or the DIAL-R, and their language level is assessed by the Zimmerman Preschool Language Scale. Vision and hearing tests are included, along with height and weight measurement.

Program Staffing

To carry out the programs, 72 members staff work 2 to 40 hours per week in a variety of positions. Teachers include people with early education, drama, science, social work, art, media, special education, speech and language, secretarial, recreation, and psychology skills. Early childhood special education staff members, district kindergarten staff members, and developmental kindergarten staff members must be certified. Parent educators undergo rigorous initial and ongoing training. Although not a requirement, a large percentage of staff members holds certification.

Program Evaluation

The program has grown from 25 children in a 3-hour preschool to 1,100 children and families involved in a wide range of services for children birth through 12 years. Enrollment increased 400 percent 1984-87.

The program was chosen for inclusion in a Public School Early Childhood Study conducted by Bank Street College and Wellesley College Center for Research on Women. Programs selected for that study had to meet the criteria of educational soundness and responsiveness to families' child care needs.

The program is licensed by the Missouri Division of Family Services and received voluntary accreditation under the auspices of the state of Missouri. The accreditation process stresses quality programs to answer the needs of children and families. The Missouri State Distinguished Service Award was presented to the center at the annual Conference on the Young Years.

Program Funding

The funding for this program comes from the state and other sources, including fees from participants. Expenditures cover salaries and benefits, supplies, administration, maintenance, and food.

Strongest Element of the Program

The unique strength of the program is the coordination, integration, and interrelationships at the site and between the two districts.

Reference

Hohmann, Mary, Bernard Banet, and David P. Weikart. *Young Children in Action: A Manual for Preschool Educators*. Ypsilanti, Mich.: High/Scope Press, 1979.

8
Resources for Public Schools

DIANNE ROTHENBERG

American Federation of Teachers
(AFT)
555 New Jersey Ave., N.W.
Washington, DC 20001
(202) 879-4400
AFT, a union of teachers, paraprofessionals, and other educational personnel, supports the concept of new initiatives in child care and development under the jurisdiction of the public schools.

Of special interest: "Starting Off Right," *American Teacher,* May 1986, pp.1, 8-9. This article features high-quality preschool programs in the public schools.

Association for Supervision and Curriculum Development
(ASCD)
125 N. West St.
Alexandria, VA 22314-2798
(703) 549-9110
In the summer of 1985, ASCD's Executive Council approved a long-range plan that included a three-year focus in the early childhood area. The purpose of the plan is to intensify Association attention to the issues related to providing quality instructional programs for children aged 3 to 7 by helping school administrators, supervisors, policy makers, and other school leaders to better meet the needs of young children.

Available from ASCD: Audiotapes of keynote speakers at the ASCD Early Childhood Education in Public Schools mini-conference; *Educational Leadership,* November 1986; *Early Childhood Education: Curriculum Organization and Classroom Management* book and filmstrip set by Barbara Day; a three-part videotape series in the area of early childhood education; and National Curriculum Study Institutes in the area of early childhood education.

Center for Policy Research in Education
(CPRE)
Eagleton Institute of Politics
Rutgers University
New Brunswick, NJ 08901

CPRE receives funding from the U.S. Department of Education and is jointly operated by the Rand Corporation, Rutgers, and the University of Wisconsin at Madison.

Available from CPRE: Young Children Face the States: Issues and Options for Early Childhood Programs by W. Norton Grubb ($4; order from CPRE; also available as ED 284 681). This study discusses the historical divisions within the early childhood education community over the purposes, methods, target populations, and administration of programs for young children; examines current state initiatives; and points out choices and issues for policymakers to consider in enacting new programs.

ERIC Clearinghouse on Elementary and Early Childhood Education
(ERIC/EECE)
University of Illinois
805 W. Pennsylvania Ave.
Urbana, IL 61801
(217)333-1386

Part of ERIC, the national information system on education, ERIC/EECE collects and disseminates information related to children's development and education through early adolescence. The Clearinghouse contributes document and journal article abstracts area to the ERIC database, prepares publications, and answers questions in its scope area.

Available from ERIC/EECE: "Resources from ERIC/EECE," a brochure describing current publications and products available from the Clearinghouse; "What Should Young Children Be Learning?", an ERIC Digest by Lilian G. Katz, Clearinghouse director (both items free upon request).

ERIC Documents: Listed below are selected ERIC Documents (EDs) on public schools and early childhood education. They can be read on microfiche in many libraries and information centers (contact ERIC/EECE for a list of ERIC microfiche collections in your state) or ordered in paper copy or microfiche from the ERIC Document Reproduction Service (EDRS), 3900 Wheeler Ave., Alexandria, VA 22304. For complete ordering information, call EDRS at (800) 227-3742, or consult the most recent issue of ERIC's monthly journal *Resources in Education*, published by the Government Printing Office; also available at many libraries. (*RIE* contains abstracts and indexes for ERIC documents. *Current Index to Journals in Education (CIJE)*, ERIC's other abstract journal [prepared by the ERIC Clearinghouses and published by ORYX Press], provides annotations and indexes for education-related journal articles.)

Early Childhood Commission. "Take a Giant Step: An Equal Start in Education for All New York City Four-Year-Olds. Final Report of the Early Childhood Education Commission." 1986.
>   Describes the work of the Commission, appointed by Mayor Edward Koch in 1985, to develop recommendations for the phased implementation of universally available preschool education for 4-year-olds starting in September 1986. Of special interest is chapter 5, which lists nine essential program components and associated rationales believed essential to accomplishing the goals of the program, and chapter 6, which provides a guide to implementation. A lengthy bibliography and charts are attached. (ED 267 911; 280 pp.)

Grace, Cathy, and Jane B. Woodruff. "The Mississippi Model— Designing and Implementing Staff Development for Statewide Implementation of Early Childhood Programs in Public Schools." 1986.
>   Describes generic guidelines followed when Mississippi planned and implemented a statewide early childhood program. According to teacher evaluations, use of the guidelines clarified program goals, improved school staff communication regarding program content and instruction of students, and helped unite early childhood educators to work for improved programs. (ED 276 697; 25 pp.)

Kansas State Department of Education. "Need and Feasibility for Early Childhood Education in the Public Schools: A Report to the Kansas State Board of Education." 1986.
>   Describes the process by which the state board of education decided that Kansas should implement early childhood education in the public schools. Includes 10 recommendations

for implementation of early childhood programs. (ED 280 581; 26 pp.)

Koppel, Sheree P., and Karen D. Isenhour. "MAP Out a Public Preschool Care and Education Plan: Multiphased Need Assessment for Program Decisions (Draft)." 1986.

Describes an assessment process using community forums, key informants, and nominal group technique. The process was used to inform decision makers of a large urban school district about the need for early childhood programs in the community. The MAP process was used to determine the types of programs wanted by the community and to coordinate community perceptions, preschool professional expertise, and parental desires in a study preliminary to preschool planning. (ED 268 174; 73 pp.)

Mitchell, Anne, and Michelle Seligson. "Early Childhood Education and the Public Schools." School Age Child Care Project, Wellesley College, 1986.

Reports preliminary findings of a new research study designed to investigate ways schools are responding to opportunities to participate in family-responsive early childhood programs. The complete report is expected in 1988. (ED 278 497; 6 pp.)

National Black Child Development Institute. "Child Care in the Public Schools: Incubator for Inequality?" 1985.

Examines the consequences, particularly for black children, of the trend toward lodging preschool care in urban public schools. Components that must be included in public-school based programs for young children are delineated and action steps are recommended. (ED 265 969; 35 pp.)

Texas Education Agency, Austin. "Priority '86: A Guide for Prekindergarten Education." 1986.

Presents ideas for implementing prekindergarten programs, including suggestions regarding developmentally appropriate curriculum, especially in the areas of developing communication, cognition, fine arts, and social-emotional skills. Also discusses guidelines for coordinating public school prekindergarten programs with existing programs like Head Start and presents specific suggestions for classroom environments. Includes information on the requirements of limited English students. (ED 271 221; 58 pp.)

Thompson, Virginia L., and Janice Molnar. "Universally-Available

Educational Programs for Four-Year-Olds: An Issue of Policy."
1986.

Examines New York City's progress in providing public
school prekindergarten programs since they were first recommended by Mayor Edward Koch in 1985. Specifically discusses
the status of efforts to implement the mayor's recommendations
and the policy issues involved in the city's implementation efforts. (ED 279 415, 23 pp.)

Wallace, Sherry. "Prekindergarten Education: Instructional Management Leads to Consistent Achievement." 1985.

Describes the Fort Worth Independent School District's
full-day prekindergarten program for 4-year-olds who scored 7
or fewer items on the Preschool Screening Evaluation (PSE).
The program, which has been in operation since 1968, is dis-
cussed in terms of staffing, numbers of children served, and
curriculum. Emphasis is on development of skills in four areas:
auditory, visual, motor, and language processes. (ED 270 214;
32 pp.)

High/Scope Educational Research Foundation
600 N. River St.
Ypsilanti, MI 48198-2898
(313) 485-2000

High/Scope is a nonprofit research, development, and training
organization with headquarters in Ypsilanti, Michigan. The Foundation's principal goals are to promote the learning and development of children from infancy through adolescence and to provide
information and training for parents and teachers. High/Scope has
conducted longitudinal research on the Ypsilanti/Perry Preschool
Project to show the long-term positive effects of high-quality programs for preschool children.

Available from High/Scope: High/Scope Resource, a guide to the
activities, products, and services of the Foundation, published three
times a year by High Scope Press, a division of the Foundation (free;
write High/Scope and request to be put on the mailing list); and
"Policy Options for Preschool Programs," by Lawrence J. Schweinhart and Jeffrey J. Koshel. (High/Scope Early Childhood Policy Papers, No.5., $5; order directly from High/Scope; also available as
ED 276 515, 45 pp.)

The National Association for the Education of Young Children
(NAEYC)
1834 Connecticut Ave., N.W.
Washington, DC 20009
(800) 424-2460

An association of more than 55,000 members, NAEYC offers a variety of services likely to be useful to public schools interested in adding an early childhood education component. NAEYC offers publications, videos, pamphlets and brochures on the education and care of children.

Available from NAEYC: "Good Teaching Practices for Four- and Five-Year-Olds" (brochure; single copies free for self-addressed, stamped envelope, or $.50 each, $10.00 for 100 copies); and "Developmentally Appropriate Practice in Early Childhood Programs: Serving Children Birth through Eight" ($5.00; Publication no. 224). Orders under $20 must be prepaid; publications catalog available upon request.

National Association of Elementary School Principals
(NAESP)
1615 Duke St.
Alexandria, VA 22314
(703) 684-3345

NAESP offered the new training program "Administration of Early Childhood Programs" as part of its National Principals Academy courses in April 1988. Planned and presented in collaboration with the High/Scope Educational Research Foundation, the workshop is being repeated on request. For more information, call NAESP or the High/Scope Developmental Services Office (313/485-2000).

NAESP is also working on guidelines for early childhood education that are expected to be ready for distribution in the summer of 1989. The guidelines are intended to help administrators establish a sound early childhood program in their schools.

National Association of State Boards of Education
(NASBE)
701 N. Fairfax, Suite 340
Alexandria, VA 22314
(703) 684-4000

In November 1987, NASBE announced plans to form a task force on early childhood education. The 25-member task force consulted with national experts at an initial meeting in Washington in February 1988 and planned to hear testimony from state policymakers and program managers at regional meetings in Atlanta, Boston, Chicago, and San Francisco in spring 1988. The group also planned to issue policy recommendations for state boards in a report to the NASBE annual conference in October 1988.

National Black Child Development Institute
(NBCDI)
1463 Rhode Island Ave., N.W.
Washington, DC 20005
(202) 387-1281

NBCDI is an advocacy organization for black children and youth. Concerned that early childhood programs in urban public schools may be inadequate to nurture black children, NBCDI has prepared a set of recommendations for successful programs.

Available from NBCDI: "Safeguards: Guidelines for Establishing Programs for Four-Year-Olds in the Public Schools." ($6; order directly from NCBDI.)

National Conference of State Legislatures
(NCSL)
1050 17th St., Suite 2100
Denver, CO 80265

NCSL operates the Child Care/Early Childhood Education Project, funded by the Carnegie Foundation to provide technical assistance to states on child care and early education issues. Funds are used to set up statewide conferences and provide testimony in state legislatures on increasing support for early childhood programs. Each year, six states are selected for technical assistance and provided with a grant by NCSL. Six states for 1987-88 (New York, Alaska, Iowa, New Hampshire, Vermont, and Tennessee) have already been selected; six more states will be chosen in fall 1988. Contact NCSL for more details.

Available from NCSL: "State Early Childhood Initiatives" (published March 1988; contact NCSL Publications Department for ordering information). This publication will provide information on funding levels, numbers of children served, special characteristics of target groups, and connections to Head Start.

North Central Regional Educational Laboratory
(NCREL)
295 Emroy Ave.
Elmhurst, IL 60126
(312) 941-7677

NCREL is a federally funded regional education laboratory that has been investigating the problem of children at risk. Besides the publication listed below, other information on this subject is available on request.

Available from NCREL: "Students at Risk: Review of Conditions, Circumstances, Indicators, and Educational Implications" by Harriett Doss Willis (Order No. SAR-701; $6.00 with check or purchase order addressed to NCREL Publications Department). Parts of the bibliography deal with preschool programs.

National Education Association
(NEA)
1201 16th St., N.W.
Washington, DC 20036
(202) 822-7200

NEA is planning projects and publications on public school involvement with early childhood education for late 1988 and 1989. The January issue of *NEA Today* (pp. 22-27) featured an article by David Elkind titled, "Educating the Very Young: A Call for Clear Thinking." The article cited three recent and forthcoming books that discuss the education of young children: *Early Schooling: The National Debate*, Sharon Lynn Kagan and Edward Zigler (New Haven: Yale University Press, 1987); *Engaging the Minds of Young Children: The Project Approach*, Lilian G. Katz and S. Chard (Norwood, N.J.: Ablex, in press); and *Miseducation: Preschoolers at Risk*, David Elkind (New York: Knopf, 1987).

The Regional Laboratory (For Educational Improvement for the Northeast and Islands)
290 S. Main St.
Andover, MA 01810
(617) 470-1080

The Regional Laboratory, operated by The Network in Andover, Massachusetts, is one of the federally funded regional education laboratories and research centers. The publication listed below is one of a series of five information packets dealing with serving at-risk children and youth.

Available from The Regional Laboratory: "Good Beginnings for Young Children: Early Identification of High Risk Youth and Programs that Promote Success" by Janet M. Thleeger ($2.25 plus $2.50 and handling; prepaid orders only; publication No. 9504). This publication is a brief overview of research with a resource bibliography that summarizes available programs for at-risk children.

Southern Association on Children Under Six
(SACUS)
Box 5403
Brady Station
Little Rock, AR 72215
(501) 227-6404

SACUS is a nonprofit professional education organization of 13,000 members. SACUS works on behalf of young children and their families. Its major functions include the dissemination of information about young children and provision of inservice development opportunities.

Available from SACUS: "Position Statement on Quality Four Year Old Programs in Public Schools" (single copies available free of charge; order directly from SACUS; also available as ED 272 272).

About the Authors

*Diane Berreth (policy panel staff liaison) is Director of Field Services, Association for Supervision and Curriculum Development, Alexandria, Virginia.

*Ada Puryear Burnette, is Administrator of Early Childhood and Elementary Education, Florida State Department of Education, Tallahassee.

Douglas Carnine is Associate Professor, College of Education, University of Oregon, Eugene.

Linda Carnine is Vice Principal, Creslane Elementary School, Eugene, Oregon.

*Milly Cowles is Distringuished Professor of Education, University of Alabama at Birmingham.

*Barbara D. Day (policy panel chair) is Professor and Chair, Department of Teaching and Learning, School of Education, University of North Carolina, Chapel Hill.

David Elkind is Professor of Child Study, Tufts University, Medford, Massachusetts.

*Russell Gersten is Professor of Education, University of Oregon, Eugene.

Joan Karp is currently a special education consultant in Eugene, Oregon; earlier, she codirected the Rhode Island Early Childhood State Plan Grant.

Lilian G. Katz is Director of the ERIC Clearinghouse on Elementary and Early Childhood Education, University of Illinois, Urbana.

*Marcia Knoll is Principal, P.S. 220 Queens, Forest Hills, New York.

*Margaret Kuypers is Director of Elementary Education and Principal, Blair Mill Elementary School, Hatboro, Pennsylvania.

*John E. Kyle (policy panel project editor) is a consultant for the Kids' Case Studies Project, National League of Cities, Washington, D.C.

Dianne Rothenberg is Associate Director of the ERIC Clearinghouse on Elementary and Early Childhood Education, University of Illinois, Urbana.

*John Varis is Superintendent, Reading Community Schools, Reading, Ohio.

*Cynthia Warger (policy panel staff liaison) is Director of Professional Development, Association for Supervision and Curriculum Development, Alexandria, Virginia.

David P. Weikart is President of the High/Scope Educational Research Foundation, Ypsilanti, Michigan.

Paul Weisberg is Professor of Psychology and Director of the Early Childhood Learning Center at the University of Alabama, Tuscaloosa.

*Verlma West is Director of Elementary Curriculum, Tulsa Public Schools, Tulsa, Oklahoma.

*Members of the ASCD Policy Panel on Early Childhood Education. Guest reviewers for the panel included Dolores Varnon, Principal, Westbriar Elementary School, Vienna, Virginia, and Charles Shepherd, Georgia Department of Education, Calhoun. Tempe Thomas served as special research assistant for the panel.